Why Six Days?

Why Six Days?

The Impact of Creation on Theology

Ronald C. Marks, Ph.D.

AnnoMundi Publishers

Whys Six Days?
The Impact of Creation on Theology
Copyright © 2018 Ronald C. Marks
All rights reserved. No part of this publication may be reproduced, stored in a retrieval system, or transmitted in any form by any means, electronic, mechanical, photocopy, recording, or otherwise, without the prior permission of the publisher, except as provided for by USA copyright law.
Cover design: Ronald C. Marks
First Printing 2018
Unless otherwise indicated, Scripture quotations are from the *ESV® Bible* (*The Holy Bible, English Standard Version®*), copyright ©2001 by Crossway, a publishing ministry of Good News Publishers. Used by permission. All rights reserved.
All emphases in Scripture quotations have been added by the author.
ISBN: 978-1732310803 (AnnoMundi Publishing)

ACKNOWLEDGMENTS

As all writers with families, I am deeply indebted to mine. First to my amazing wife, Joann for her patience and encouragement. Thank you, Joann, for the uncounted hours of assistance in intellectual, theological, and personal advice and counsel. Thank you, Rebekah, for all the historical and theological research and assistance. Thank you both for your love and compassion.

I am grateful to the work of God through so many others in the Body of Christ. I have seen far only by standing on the shoulders of giants.

Soli Deo Gloria

Contents

Chapter 1 Not Another Book About Young-Earth Creation! 1
    The Amazing Claim in Isaiah 6

Chapter 2 The Question 11
    Evolution takes hold 12
    Evolution gains ground 13
    Evolution challenged 14
    Why Six Days? 17

Chapter 3 The Hermeneutic Shuffle 19
    Establishing a Good Hermeneutic 20
    A Good Hermeneutic Proposed 21
    Avoiding the Hermeneutic Shuffle 22

Chapter 4 Wrong Answers 29
    Isn't This Just Allegory? 30
    What About Chance? 33
    A Few Wrong Answers 37

Chapter 5 Applying the Non-shuffling, Really Good Hermeneutic. 41

Chapter 6 God Expects His People to Understand 47

Chapter 7 The Pattern 53
    It's in The Ten Commandments 56
    It is Much More than The Ten Commandments 59
    The Pattern in the Flood of Noah 59
    Between Deliverance from Egypt and the Giving of the Law 63

Chapter 8 The Pattern Emphasized 65
    The Sabbath Year 66
    The Seven Sevens and Jubilee 68

Chapter 9 The Pattern in Fulfillment 73
    The Appearance Feasts 74
    Passover 76

    Unleavened Bread 77
    Beginning of the Harvest or First Fruits 78
    Pentecost (The Feast of Weeks) 79
    Feast of Trumpets 82
    Yom Kippur 83
    Sukkoth 84

Chapter 10 The Sabbath Has a Purpose, Too 89
    The Sabbath is Part of the Creation 91
    God Rested on the Sabbath 94
    A Sovereign Creator 95
    Rest Teaches About Salvation 97
    Israel Left Bondage in Egypt for the Promised Land 99

Chapter 11 An Answer 105
    The Days of Creation 106
    The Millennium was Foretold 107
    The Remarkable Confession of Job 114
    The Disciples Looked for a Real, Physical Kingdom 116
    Is A Thousand, A Thousand? 118
    What Does This Mean? 120

Chapter 12 Who Else Believes This is the Answer? 125
    Early Church Fathers 126
    The Epistle of Barnabas (100 – 130 A.D.) 127
    Hippolytus of Rome (170 – 235 A.D.) 129
    Lucius Caecilius Firmianus Lactantius (250 – 325) 130
    Augustine of Hippo (354 – 430 A.D.) 132
    Pre-Modern Theologians 134
    Alfonso X of Castile and Leon (1221 – 1284) 134
    Christopher Columbus 135
    Recent Theologians 137
    Other Modern Theologians 140

Chapter 13 Living In Light of the Lord's Return 141

About the Author 155

וַיְהִי עֶרֶב וַיְהִי בֹקֶר יוֹם הַשִּׁשִּׁי

And there was evening and there was morning, a sixth day

וַיְכֻלּוּ הַשָּׁמַיִם וְהָאָרֶץ וְכָל צְבָאָם

The heavens and the earth were finished, the whole host of them

וַיְכַל אֱלֹהִים בַּיּוֹם הַשְּׁבִיעִי מְלַאכְתּוֹ אֲשֶׁר עָשָׂה

And on the seventh day God completed his work that he had done

וַיִּשְׁבֹּת בַּיּוֹם הַשְּׁבִיעִי מִכָּל מְלַאכְתּוֹ אֲשֶׁר עָשָׂה

and he rested on the seventh day from all his work that he had done

וַיְבָרֶךְ אֱלֹהִים אֶת יוֹם הַשְּׁבִיעִי וַיְקַדֵּשׁ אֹתוֹ

And God blessed the seventh day, and sanctified it

כִּי בוֹ שָׁבַת מִכָּל מְלַאכְתּוֹ אֲשֶׁר בָּרָא אֱלֹהִים לַעֲשׂוֹת

because in it he had rested from all his work that God had created to do

בָּרוּךְ אַתָּה יְיָ אֱלֹהֵינוּ מֶלֶךְ הָעוֹלָם

Blessed are you, Lord, our God, sovereign of the universe

בּוֹרֵא פְּרִי הַגָּפֶן (אמן)

Who creates the fruit of the vine (Amen)

בָּרוּךְ אַתָּה יְיָ אֱלֹהֵינוּ מֶלֶךְ הָעוֹלָם

Blessed are You, Lord, our God, King of the Universe

אֲשֶׁר קִדְּשָׁנוּ בְּמִצְוֹתָיו וְרָצָה בָנוּ

who sanctifies us with his commandments, and has been pleased with us

וְשַׁבָּת קָדְשׁוֹ בְּאַהֲבָה וּבְרָצוֹן הִנְחִילָנוּ זִכָּרוֹן לְמַעֲשֵׂה בְרֵאשִׁית

You have lovingly and willingly given us Your holy Shabbat as an inheritance, in memory of creation

כִּי הוּא יוֹם תְּחִלָּה לְמִקְרָאֵי קֹדֶשׁ זֵכֶר לִיצִיאַת מִצְרָיִם

because it is the first day of our holy assemblies, in memory of the exodus from Egypt

כִּי בָנוּ בָחַרְתָּ וְאוֹתָנוּ קִדַּשְׁתָּ מִכָּל הָעַמִּים

because You have chosen us and made us holy from all peoples

וְשַׁבַּת קָדְשְׁךָ בְּאַהֲבָה וּבְרָצוֹן הִנְחַלְתָּנוּ

and have willingly and lovingly given us Your holy Shabbat for an inheritance

בָּרוּךְ אַתָּה יְיָ מְקַדֵּשׁ הַשַּׁבָּת (אמן)

Blessed are You, who sanctifies Shabbat (Amen)

---

[1] Kiddush is a blessing recited to sanctify the Sabbath and other Jewish holidays. Kiddush means "sanctification". Note the statement regarding the Sabbath and creation.

CHAPTER 1
NOT ANOTHER BOOK ABOUT YOUNG-EARTH CREATION!

We could blame Charles Darwin. If we must blame someone or anyone for the interest among both Christians and non-Christians concerning the age of the earth, certainly, Charles Darwin would be on the short list. Even though the age of the earth has been a topic of

---

[2] Frontpiece to the book of Genesis from the Maklinburg Bible By Phillip Medhurst (Photos by Harry Kossuth) [Public domain], via Wikimedia Commons, https://upload.wikimedia.org/wikipedia/commons/b/b3/Vignette_by_Loutherbourg_for_the_Macklin_Bible_133_of_134._Bowyer_Bible_New_Testament._Headpiece_to_Revelations.gif

human conversation from at least the time of Plato. And, I suspect since the first humans were on the earth. Perhaps there was a conversation even between the first two humans that went something like this:

"Adam, how old is the earth?", asked Eve. "Let's see", Adam replied. "God created the heavens and the earth in six days, rested on the seventh, we sinned and were kicked out of the Garden of Eden on the eighth. It's been two days since we were kicked out. That makes today the eleventh day since God started creating. The world is eleven days old." Eve looked up at the stars and said, "Then how can we see that star over there that scientists tell us is 4.5 million light-years away? And, who are our children going to marry?"

Of the multitude of humans who have walked on this earth since the creation, at least a few have wondered and hypothesized about the age of the earth. Western European intellectuals, thoroughly marinated in a Judeo-Christian worldview, attempted to calculate the age of the earth using the genealogies in Genesis matched to historic events. In addition to Ussher's calculated age of the earth[3], we can add those who affirmed a literal reading of the Genesis chronologies Moses ben Maimon (often referred to as simply Maimonides)[4], Isaac Newton[5], Johannes Kepler, King Alfonso[6], and many others. In addition to these

---

[3] James Ussher's well-known age of the earth is 4004 B.C. More precisely, October 23, 4004 B.C. He published this date with the underlying determination in *Annales Veteris Testamenti, a prima mundi origine deducti, una cum rerum Asiaticarum et Aegyptiacarum chronico, a temporis historici principio usque ad Maccabaicorum initia producto*. ("Annals of the Old Testament, deduced from the first origins of the world, the chronicle of Asiatic and Egyptian matters together produced from the beginning of historical time up to the beginnings of Maccabees"), published in 1650.

[4] Rabbi Moses ben Maimon calculated a date of 4058 B.C.

[5] Isaac Newton stated the age of the earth was revealed in Scripture, using that age to show excessive ages in the chronologies of other kingdoms, in *The Chronology of Ancient Kingdoms Amended. To which is Prefix'd, a Short Chronicle from the First Memory of Things in Europe, to the Conquest of Persia by Alexander the Great*. Published posthumously, London, 1728, Project Gutenberg edition, http://www.gutenberg.org/ebooks/15784.

[6] Christopher Columbus actually incorporated the calculation of King Alfonso X of Castile (November 23, 1221 – April 4, 1284) in Columbus' *Book of Prophecies*, 1501, English Translation by Kay Brigham, 2001, p. 181.

scholars who understood the historic passages in the Bible as depicting real history were others who calculated the age using a non-literal reading of Genesis. With the publication in November 1859 of Darwin's *magnum opus*, *On the Origin of Species by Means of Natural Selection, or the Preservation of Favored Races in the Struggle for Life*, a tectonic shift in the intellectual foundation of the age of the earth emerged. Darwin's book became the nexus for our culture's beliefs regarding any human origin apologetic. Bible-believing Christians responded through sermons, books, letters-to-the-editor, theme parks and museums, public presentations and producing videos. Proponents of an old-earth defined by atheistic science have succeeded in controlling the narrative in public education and cultural entertainment.

What if Darwin hadn't put forth his theories? What if the ideas of evolution or any other scientific revelation had not challenged the Biblical record of creation? Would Christians care about the age of the earth? Would it matter if we believe the world was only about 6,000 years old? I addressed one aspect of this in "Does It Matter?"[7] That presentation addressed the consequences of real events occurring in real space and placed in real time as described in the Genesis account of creation. Some Christians who wonder if we should be investing resources in defending our views on the creation of the earth when the Gospel message still needs to be preached. Or, they just can't be bothered to care about whether Adam and Eve were real, literal people who existed in real space and real time when their mother is suffering from Alzheimer's, or their best friend is addicted to pornography and getting a divorce from his spouse of 20 years. Life is too complex and hard. We just don't have time to add one more distraction to our list.

The complexities of our modern world and modern lives make thinking about the age of the earth as "too mundane." Too monotone in our symphonic lives. For the modern (or, even post-modern)

---

[7] Available online at https://youtu.be/3AndGNyRVJ8, as of January 17, 2018.

Christians, the age of the earth discussion is as exciting as an analogue TV show in a 4K streaming world.

Here's the first of bad news. It isn't. The age of the earth isn't mundane or unimportant. It doesn't detract from Gospel work. The age of the earth isn't just about whether the world is 6,000 years old or 4.5 billion years old. There may be well-placed concerns that some young-earth advocates have become near-sighted and beginnings-focused. Perhaps in our defense, we would note that while we are working hard to defend the Biblical account of creation against the world-wide flood of evolutionary dogma, we can both become and appear singularly focused on this issue. The perception we only care about defending a young-earth will get in the way of the message.

More "bad news" for the age-agnostic. It matters to the Gospel. Young earth creation has been accused of neglecting the Gospel while simultaneously accused of requiring belief in a young-earth as a component of salvation. Aside from being contradictory, neither are true. In order to have a consistent young-earth creation view, the Gospel must be more than just present. The Gospel must have priority. A young-earth view that is consistent with the rest of theology confesses a literal reading of Genesis reveals a literal Jesus as Creator, Who is the same literal Jesus revealed throughout the remainder of scripture as Lord and Savior. Our Savior is The Creator.[8]

A Biblical view of Genesis, meaning one that confesses a literal-historical view of Genesis, is filled with confession of the ultimate authorship of Creation in the hands of the Creator. Because Jesus is the

---

[8] It is significant that the Gospel of John begins by claiming that Jesus is God and present from eternity past. Jesus, Christ is identified as the eternally present person of the Trinity whom was the principal person responsible for the creation: "In the beginning was the Word, and the Word was with God, and the Word was God. He was in the beginning with God. All things were made through him, and without him was not any thing made that was made. In him was life, and the life was the light of men." John 1:1-4 English Standard Version

Creator, He is the self-revealing author Who also entered His creation to live a revelatory life. In all that He does, He retains ultimate authority.

Even though young-earth Christians make this connection of Creator-Savior, and apply this connection of Jesus throughout scripture, most young-earth creation presentations, or videos, or books, emphasize the science-based apologetic. The result is a message that the young-earth position has been sufficiently addressed by the scientific evidence that refutes evolution or indicates a limited age of 6,000 years. And, with most of the effort directed toward convincing or equipping others to hold and defend the Biblical view of a young earth, we are satisfied that we have done our duty.

Yet, many Christians who are conservative in their theology, even reformed in their theology, have never considered the impact of what six days of creation *mean*. Six days followed by a day of rest is assumed and then lifted out of Genesis as a reason we have a week of seven days. Christians may carefully ensure they celebrate "The Lord's Day" every seven days, but do so without wondering "why?" beyond that fact that we do. For this Christian, there is nothing important or valuable in the quantity of days. Nothing here that will impact their lives, their church,

their culture. There is no reason to consider the answer to this question, "why six days followed by a day of rest?".

Why six days? Why did God specifically and intentionally choose to create everything in six days, and then set aside the seventh day and particularly mark it as "His" day?

The Amazing Claim in Isaiah

The prophet Isaiah is responsible for one of the larger Old Testament prophetic books. The name "Isaiah" means "The Lord is Salvation". You may be thinking "what has that got to do with the question of days?" Give me, and yourself, some grace to realize God doesn't do anything by accident. Is God a God of purpose? Or, is He under the control of circumstances? Could God ordain and cause a man to be named "Isaiah" in order to communicate something to us? To answer, "perhaps" indicates a very small view of God. There is meaning even in the name. And, there is meaning that may help understand the message of this prophet.

In addition to this important and specific name, Isaiah is directly quoted more often in the New Testament than any other Old Testament prophet.[9] He lived and prophesied when the nation of Israel was divided into two kingdoms. The northern kingdom of Israel containing most of the tribes, and the southern kingdom of Judah. Much of the prophecies can be characterized as "condemnation of the empty ritualism of his day and the idolatry into which so many of the people had fallen."[10] This same warning could be given to the church throughout its history. Perhaps, it is useful to the church today.

As a prophet of God, Isaiah warned of an impending judgement that would include the taking of the Jewish people into Babylonian captivity.

---

[9] John MacArthur, "The MacArthur Study Bible", Introductory notes to the book of Isaiah, Thomas Nelson Publishers, 1997, p. 952.
[10] MacArthur, p. 953

God made sure that in addition to this warning of judgement for their sins He also gave hope and encouragement to His people that the captivity would come to an end. God made sure the Nation of Israel knew the judgement was coming and it would have an end. He used Isaiah to identify the Persian King Cyrus as the one who would be the instrument of God in the restoration from the Babylonian exile.

God's judgement was just. It was harsh judgement because it was fitting to the sin they had committed. God in His graciousness was reminding them that even though judgement was coming, it would also come to an end. The judgement was not final. There was a restoration to come.

The warning of judgement was given first, followed by the promise of restoration and a picture of the salvation of God. It is in the promise of restoration that we find an amazing claim. As the salvation of God is revealed, Isaiah writes of the character of God that both shows Who God Is and reminds of What God has done and is doing.

> *"Remember this and stand firm, recall it to mind, you transgressors, remember the former things of old; for I am God, and there is no other; I am God, and there is none like me, declaring the end from the beginning and from ancient times things not yet done, saying, 'My counsel shall stand, and I will accomplish all my purpose,' calling a bird of prey from the east, the man of my counsel from a far country. I have spoken, and I will bring it to pass; I have purposed, and I will do it.*[11]

God compares Himself to the false gods who have no power, no ability to save. False gods are powerless because they are false gods. The real God has all power, knowledge, ability because He is The Real God. God could have revealed this by saying many things. But, He does so

---

[11] Isaiah 46:8-11

Why Six Days?

in this way. What way? By claiming that only He has the ability to declare "the end from the beginning". What are we to make of this?

This claim is no boast. God does not state He can declare the end from the beginning, but that He *does* declare the end from the beginning.

If God meant that only He knows certain things, then why isn't that what He said? If we want to believe this means God is able to know things in the future before they actually occur, then we must explain why this particular claim is used. God could have said very clearly "I proclaim what has not yet come to pass." Or, He could have said, "I know what's going to happen even before it does happen." Or, He could have said anything that would mean "He knows the future". He didn't. He said this. He claims to have *declared* the end from the beginning.

The word translated as "end" is the Hebrew אחרית (*akh-ar-eeth'*), meaning the *last* or *end*. Or, something yet in the *future*, but also the culmination of future things. The clear meaning being "the last". If God meant something other than what is clearly stated, He is able to say whatever that was. We don't need to speculate for Him what He meant to say. He said, "I declare the end from the beginning."

The New American Standard Bible translation, this word *akhareeth* is translated as "the end" 20 times, and "future" 7 times. The context is essential for understanding the meaning, and Isaiah helps us know which meaning is best suited here. God used the word translated "the beginning", and placed it here with the word translated as "the end." That's the correct meaning. "The end".

He follows this with another statement, an emphasis, in which He specifically claims the ability to describe the future. Thus, "declaring the end from the beginning" is not a statement that God knows the future, or can tell us about the future. It clearly means he is declaring the end from the beginning.

So, let's ask, "What end?" "What beginning?" Certainly, God is declaring the end of judgement from the beginning of judgement. But, that's not the purpose of this claim. This claim is the confidence that God can declare the end of the judgement because He has declared the end of something else already from the beginning of that same thing. He has declared the end of the earth from the beginning of the earth.

What is declared at the beginning?
- Seven definite periods of time. Seven days. Distinct in number.
- Seven distinct periods of time that are in sequence.
- Distinct items clearly divided into a group of six and a seventh.
- Each day having a distinct purpose in revealing the work of God.

Why Six Days?

CHAPTER 2
THE QUESTION

Like many other Christians in conservative Christian homes or attending moderate to conservative churches, I was constantly exposed to Biblical truth. The churches I attended and the Christians I was exposed to represented what I was sure were "just slightly above average" Christians. I heard the story of Zacchaeus climbing into the tree to see Jesus pass by[12] so many times it had become tiresome. The stories of creation and the nation of Israel, along with the judges (who couldn't admire and loath and grieve for Sampson?) were well known. I heard of Job's trial and triumph without ever really understanding what or why. But, I knew them, along with the amazing accounts of Daniel, Elijah, and Elisha. And, of course, the New Testament Gospels were never ending sources of understanding God's Gospel foretold, fulfilled, and applied.

Yet, Genesis and the age of the earth weren't talked about very much. The movies, TV, and even popular music, the public schools, and the culture all sent a very clear message: Evolution was the explanation of how things came to be. Animals had evolved from other

---

[12] If you are not familiar with this story, you can find it in the Gospel of Luke 19:1-10.

animals and from pre-animals. Humans had a common ancestor with other animals that included most recently a common ancestor with apes. Mary Leakey was making her discoveries, and the "out of Africa" hypothesis was gaining footholds in science while also making advances in the public conscious.

Evolution takes hold

My first three years of undergraduate education were at a Christian college in Arizona. In those years, the college was owned and operated by the Arizona Southern Baptists. Although I began my undergraduate degree by declaring a pastoral-related major, I changed in the middle of my third semester while taking my first chemistry class. The amazing complexity and interdependency of atoms and molecules, as well as the subatomic particles called out as evidence of an intelligent Creator. I was enthralled and became convinced that God wanted me to become a chemist. I reasoned that He could then use the skills He had given me to understand science to open doors normally closed. Who knows? Maybe being a chemist, I could go to nations closed to missionary work as a "missionary *incognito*". My profession of Christian service merged with my ability and new-found love for science.

I had Christian teachers. Or, at least they seemed to be Christians. There were only three science faculty: a biologist, a chemist, and a physicist. As with many small school with a desire to grow, this school had more students than their faculty could support. Time to hire more. The chemistry professor asked several of his students to give their opinions of a candidate who would become another chemistry professor. This candidate was great at teaching, seemed to know what he needed to know (from our very innocent perspective), and mentioned during the interview that he held to a young-earth view. The other chemist – the one who had taught my classes and gained my respect – he scoffed at the statement. After the candidate had left, my professor made some indirect remarks to us to the effect that holding a young-earth view significantly impacted the credentials of this candidate, and that he had no respect for this candidate simply because of the young-earth view. The candidate wasn't hired. I, and my classmates, became infected by those events.

The infection grew. It strengthened my position that God must have used evolution to do His creative acts. Clearly, I thought, evolution was what intellectual Christians believed. Like many other fellow Christians, I had unintentionally become a theistic evolutionist. Not intentionally. Not rationally. Simply by going along with the flow of the culture while safely in the boat of a Christian community. Not because I went to a secular or state-owned school system. I was in the "orthodox" confines of a Christian education institution. Yet, my belief that God used evolution were established and strengthened. Or, more precisely yet unknowingly, I had given science authority over scripture as the source of what was true. I had done so with regard to the creation. But, was that the only area?

Evolution gains ground

After three years at the Christian university in Arizona, I transferred to The University of Tennessee (UTK) in Knoxville. In addition to the culture shock, there was a significant social shock. The school in Arizona had 600 students. There were approximately 4,000 at the Knoxville, Tennessee campus.

Fortunately, most of my school credits transferred. Having now declared a major in chemistry, there were many courses ahead. Most of my core courses were complete, with the notable exception of needing a foreign language and a few additional science courses. I signed up for the mandatory psychology course, Russian as the foreign language (a great choice for chemists), and an anthropology course. While my church ignored specific teaching about Genesis and creation, the anthropology course was very clear. Humans had evolved, and scientists could explain this evolution. The anthropology course introduced and explained the *australopithecine* fossils along with other hominids. It was clear and unambiguous. The professor taught without apology. I took it all in and passed the course while unintentionally failing the Truth.

Once again, I chose to believe that God must have used evolution as the tool in His creation. It wasn't until much later I discovered this was not only bad science, it was really awful theology.

I had read Genesis, and would read it again during this time of studying in college. But, I never studied it. Never took the time to learn from it and give it the value I was giving to the other subjects I was learning. It has value. But, somehow, that value was different. And that made the way I understood the truth acceptable. Sure, I knew it was the word of God. "Yes", I would have answered the question, "Do you believe the Bible is the inspired word of God?" I would have even agreed that it was infallible and without error.

Not that I was theologically ignorant. When I could, I would continue to read and study theology. I struggled to learn theology proper, ecclesiology, eschatology, and the other "ologies". I purchased books on theology, including a multi-volume set by Lewis Sperry Chafer.[13] But, when it came to anthropology and origins, I read into the school lessons what I thought had to be true. Not what was true. What I thought must be true because we had to trust science. And, none of my pastors through the years had made this a very important issue. Why should I?

Evolution challenged

Those last two years at the University of Tennessee were also my first two years of my military career. I was given the opportunity to enter the military, and signed all the paperwork to enter a commissioning program through the Air Force Reserve Officer

---

[13] **No. I am not a Dispensationalist.**

The Question

Training Corps at the University of Tennessee. Upon graduation, I was given a commission as an officer in the United States Air Force, and began my career. A few years in, I received an invitation to compete for a position to teach chemistry at the United States Air Force Academy. They military would pay for my Master's Degree, and I would get to teach. What an incredible opportunity. I jumped at it.

After completing the Master's program, I arrived at the Air Force Academy and began teaching. There I met Ken. Ken was on his second tour at the Academy. He was finishing is doctoral degree while teaching. And, Ken was an ardent young-earth creationist.

Ken wasn't harsh. He wasn't pushy. Ken simply would ask questions that helped reveal my real ignorance about the creation-evolution question. His questions gently opened my mind to the fact that I had been negligent of studying an issue that I claimed to know. When I stated that God had used evolution, I had no Biblical or scientific reason to do so. It was a default position I had assumed while attempting to compromise two conflicting ideas: God created the earth versus the earth evolved out of existing chaotic matter. Two views in opposition: God, with extreme purpose and intention, created mankind versus mankind evolved from un-purposed, unintentional evolutionary events. I had taken two totally contradictory explanations of the origin of humanity, and simply slapped them together like I was making a peanut-butter and jelly sandwich. Who cares if they didn't mix. It worked for me. And, I love peanut-butter and jelly sandwiches.

Yet, the conflict began to take hold. The two incompatible views of creation began to let me know they were not happy living in the same mind. I began talking to my wife about it. She listened, helped, and one day asked me the question. Not "a", "The". If God had created in anything other than six days, then, why did He say He created in six days? Why six days?

I was stuck. While both my wife and Ken may have meant something else, I was struck by the need to answer the question of the

Why Six Days?

number of days. It was a very difficult problem. In case you've missed it, let me walk you through my thinking:

God could have created in any way He wanted to. He's God. He could have used evolution. He could have done it in one day. Because He is God, He could have created everything that exists in a single event in the smallest possible time we can imagine. But, He didn't. He chose to create in six days. And very specifically and purposefully told us He created in six days. Why then did He choose to reveal that He had done it in six days, followed by a day of rest? If He had chosen to do it by evolution, why didn't He say that, instead?

God clearly and precisely stated there was a first day. He called it the first day, or day one. That means it was the first day as in there can never be another first day. Just like there was a first day of my life. My life had a very clear and distinct beginning that can be identified as a real day. So was this first day of creation. My life had a first day. Creation had a first day. A real, twenty-four hour day.

God then clearly and precisely stated there was a second day. It was unique and distinct from the first day. God did things in the second day that were not done in the first day, and not done in any following day.

These two days were followed by a clear and precise third day that was distinct and different from the first and second. God did things on the third day that were not done on any other day. Why would He be doing this? Why would He say He had done these things if He really did something else (like evolution)?

And, God used words to describe these days that are very personal to the days. The first day has an identity as the first day. It is treated in Genesis as a unique day in that there will never be another day like this. That level of specificity is followed in every other day of creation through the seventh day. They are clearly identified as cycles of light and dark. They are treated as clearly understandable days. Why would God make this distinction if He didn't do it this way?

The Question

Why Six Days?

Young Earth Creationists generally understand the importance of "the beginning". We believe it. We research it. We talk about it to one another, and often to anyone else. We do this because we understand the importance of getting the beginning right. We understand the impact of a literal, historical, real narrative of Genesis 1-11 on the Gospel and on all of theology. Or, at least, most of theology.

However, just as the Gospel is more than a conversion experience, just as the Gospel impacts everything in our lives from how we raise our children to how we drive our cars (at least, it should), so does the answer to this question. "Why six days followed by a day of rest?"

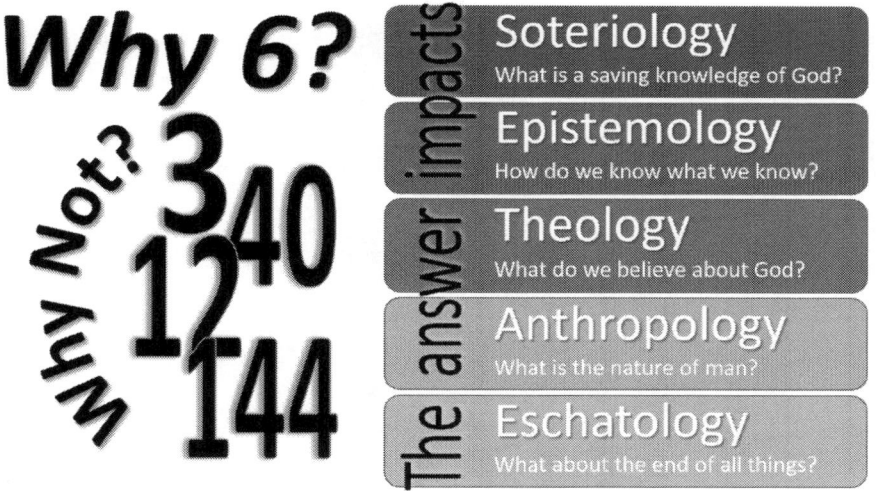

Figure 1 The answer to "Why Six Days?" Impacts all of theology.

Why six? God could have used any other number. There are so many numbers in scripture that seem to have some significance. Why not one of these? For example: Three is the number of the trinity. Jesus, after being crucified and buried, arose from being dead on the third day. Three would be a good number, it seems.

The Jews wandered in the wilderness 40 years. Noah's flood began with a rain and water event that lasted 40 days and 40 nights. Forty would have been a good number. Why not create in 40 days?

Twelve is a great number. There are twelve tribes of Israelites (from the twelve sons of Jacob), twelve disciples of Jesus, twelve gates in the new Jerusalem[14].

In the Revelation, we are told about a number of people set apart for a specific work. This number is twelve-twelves thousand, or 144 thousand.

God could choose any number, and the choosing as well as the choice be filled with extreme purpose. Therefore, our answer to this question impacts every area of how we think and live. Just as our understanding of the Gospel impacts every area of how we think and live.

The answer to "Why Six Days?" is both a reflection of your theology, and will have an impact on your theology. The answer reveals what you believe about what is true and correct, and it will mold what you believe is true and correct. Just as whether we hold to a literal view of Genesis as a historical narrative, or that Genesis is something other, the answer to "Why Six Days?" impacts all of theology. What we believe about salvation (soteriology) and the processes by which God reveals and imparts salvation. What we believe about knowledge (epistemology), and arrive at answers to the question of "What do we know and how do we know it?". What we believe about God Himself (theology proper), including His character, attributes, actions. It affects our view of mankind (anthropology) and the process of studying ourselves, our nature, our purpose. And, finally, it will impact our view of the end of things (eschatology).

---

[14] Revelation 21:9-14

CHAPTER 3
THE HERMENEUTIC SHUFFLE

You may already be thinking of an answer. Or, at least, beginning to wonder if you might know. However, rushing to an answer will keep us from seeing the real value of the answer. So, let's take an important pause in your journey to the answer for a critical confession.

How we answer this question *will impact* which of the available answers to this question we come to. It will determine if we get this answer right.

How we mine for the information used to answer this question impacts, and may change, the answer. We are going to use a method, or a system, to "pull out"

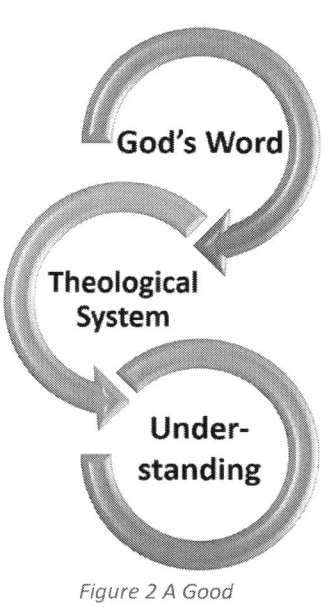

Figure 2 A Good Hermeneutic System

information from various places and then use another method to piece these information pieces back together. We have a system. All of us.

Why Six Days?

Yes, you, too. That method or system is a *hermeneutic*. Most of the time, our hermeneutic is something we use without realizing we are using it. Or, if we are aware, we may not fully appreciate the impact on the quality, trustworthiness, and accuracy of the answer.

Establishing a Good Hermeneutic

We cannot choose to have **no** hermeneutic, because that choice is itself a hermeneutic. We will always be using a hermeneutic. That's an important first step. Confess we have a method. Once we've acknowledged we have a hermeneutic, the next step is to assess it. We must check our method, or hermeneutic, to make sure it is the best we can bring to the question. After evaluating our hermeneutic for trustworthiness and appropriateness, we must intentionally and carefully work to apply the necessary tools of the hermeneutic throughout the journey to the answer.

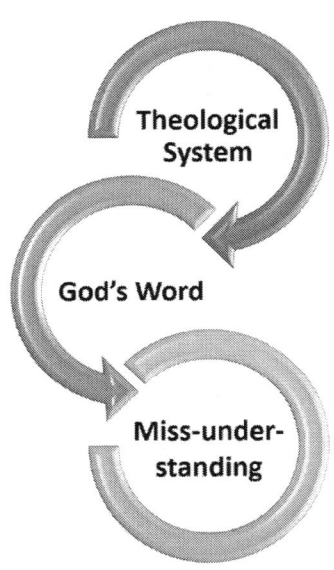

Figure 3 A Dangerous Hermeneutic System

A theological system when applied to answering questions is a hermeneutic. An excellent hermeneutic begins by acknowledging that God's Word is the source of knowledge and truth. It confesses that God's word contains correct, understandable, reliable truth. Therefore, we need a theological system that is intentionally subordinate to God's Word to gain understanding of that truth. If our theological system takes authority over God's Word, then our system becomes the source of truth instead of God's Word, and we will get wrong information, wrong understanding, and wrong answers.

This isn't as easy as it may seem. Christian history is filled with errors and even heresy that resulted from placing a theological system above God's Word, and then using the ideas and concepts of that system to form understanding from God's Word. The good news is those errors were corrected by other Christians who held God's Word as highest authority, insisting that God's Word form and change our theological system.

A Good Hermeneutic Proposed

A good and proper theological system is built from truth that is already present in God's Word. Here are some of the essential components of a good hermeneutic to be used in an excellent theology:

1. God is God. He is uncaused. He has no source, and nothing pre-exists Him. There is much more to this statement than we first comprehend. Since God is, then all that He is must also come from being all that He is. Anything that makes God smaller, or more human, or more "man-like" isn't confessing that God is God. Open theism, or openness theology,[15] is an example of a system that has lost the understanding of God as God.

2. God is Sovereign. Right. Got that. But, the consequences of a sovereign God are not always understood or incorporated into our thinking. A sovereign God does what He wants to do. We don't "allow" Him to do something or anything. Everything that is done or exists or can be imagined is because He purposed for it to be done, exist, or occur. We could have said it this way, "anything He chooses to do". However, in today's post-modern

---

[15] "In Open Theism, the future is either knowable or not knowable. For the open theists who hold that the future is knowable by God, they maintain that God voluntarily limits His knowledge of free will choices so that they can remain truly free. Other open theists maintain that the future, being nonexistent, is not knowable, even by God." (Matt Slick, "What is Open Theism", https://carm.org/what-is-open-theism, Christian Apologetics & Research Ministry, accessed July 14, 2017)

and secular-infused culture, choosing is often understood in a subordinate manner. If God wanted to create the universe over a period of billions of years, He can. If he choose to create it over a period of six seconds five days ago, he can. Regardless or any other factor. He isn't controlled by outside forces or universal laws. Similarly, God isn't controlled by hierarchy of order. He could have created the most complex thing first, and then made all the simple things later. He doesn't have to follow some hierarchy of order in creation. He determines the order. He is sovereign. We are not. Neither is order, or physics, or space, or time, or the universe, or anything sovereign over Him.
3. God is omnipotent. God can do anything He wants to do. He has all power. He could create everything that is instantaneously. He doesn't need to "pace" Himself, or wait for certain events or things to occur. When God "bakes" a cake, He doesn't have to wait for the chemicals to undergo any change. He creates the change.
4. God is the ultimate communicator. His knowledge, skill, and ability in communicating are beyond our ability to comprehend. All we can comprehend is that His ability to communicate is so advanced, so "God-like", that we cannot comprehend its limit. Only that it is exceptionally greater than any human ability.

Do you see it? God can say anything He wants to say. He is all-powerful. All-knowing. The perfect and perfectly capable communicator. Since these are all true, why did He say that He created in six days followed by a day of rest if that is not what He exactly meant to say?

Avoiding the Hermeneutic Shuffle

There is a correlation between theological systems and being "young-earth." The term "theological systems" is in reference to specific systems such as Dispensational, Reformed, Covenant, New-Covenant, or any other clearly identifiable system.

Any system which confesses that scripture speaks clearly, plainly, and obviously regarding the sovereignty of God in the salvation process, of the depravity of man and an individual's inability to contribute to the saving process, does so based on a confession that God's Word is clear and plain and obvious. Often, though not always, if a theologian believes God's Word is clear, plain, and obvious, this includes the creation events described in Genesis. Therefore, these systems correlate with a young-earth belief, and a creation in six literal days. Reformed theology stands out as being consistent in its description of God and conclusion of a young-earth. However, just because a theologian is Reformed does not mean they are young-earth.[16] And, though reformed theology contains an excellent hermeneutic regarding God's Word, this hermeneutic is not consistently applied from Genesis to Revelation.

A young-earth theological system characterizes the first chapters of Genesis as plain, clear, and obvious. In doing so, it uses a hermeneutic of exegeting the historical narrative contained in these passages. A consistent historical narrative is foundational and essential to properly and fully understand the doctrines of marriage, the trinity, identity of male and female, establishment of the family, and many other truths.

However, pulling out the correct meaning of God's Word doesn't happen by accident. Still, theologians (including this one) can become inattentive or lazy in careful and consistently applying the hermeneutic from the start of God's Word to form a theological system that exegetes

---

[16] Timothy Keller is considered by many to be reformed in his theology. However, he is an old-earth creationist. He makes the following statement which equates of incorporates evolution in the creation of man: *"Belief in evolution can be compatible with a belief in a historical fall and a literal Adam and Eve. There are many unanswered questions around this issue."* from
https://www.thegospelcoalition.org/article/sinned-in-a-literal-adam-raised-in-a-literal-christ/, accessed May 2, 2018.

the historical and literal truth from Genesis 1 through Genesis 11 without change until the end of Revelation.

Here's the problem. All theological systems can suffer from a hermeneutic shuffle. This shuffle happens when we apply the hermeneutic in one place in scripture, but not in all. Or the opposite. The hermeneutic is carefully applied everywhere with the notable exception of specific portion of scripture. That portion is Genesis 1-11.

No theologian or Christian will overtly admit they shuffle their hermeneutic to make scripture say what they hope it says, or want it to say. They can shuffle accidently. The hermeneutic shuffle is most often an unintentional occurrence. It is unacknowledged. For example, the events recorded in the Gospel of Matthew, chapter 28, are accepted as a real, historical record of the account of the resurrection of Jesus because that's what the story says. But, we then turn to Genesis chapter 2 regarding the creation of man and conclude it is analogy for no other reason than we need the earth to be older than 6,000 years. Or, that Genesis chapters 6, 7, and 8 only refer to a local flood, or not a real flood at all. Instead of a literal, historical flood, we use a hermeneutic to claim the story is for illustration of some other spiritual truth. Even though the details of the events in each of the Genesis passages are written as real, historical events.

Why the shuffle? In some cases, the reason is embedded in an unacknowledged fear of man that eclipses our fear of God.

It's not enough to have a good hermeneutic or even an excellent one. We must also be on constant guard that we do not shuffle from a hermeneutic controlled by the Biblical text into one controlled by a theological system. God's Word must inform our theological system so that we pull out the correct meaning from scripture. In this way, we protect what is understood to be true.

Think you've got that? Let's take a test. No. Don't pass this up. You'll want to know the result before going any further. You really want to take this test.

The Hermeneutic Shuffle

Do you have a good hermeneutic? Would the most theologically careful and studious Christians you know agree that it is a good hermeneutic? What does that hermeneutic produce when applied to the following scripture?

> *In the beginning was the Word, and the Word was with God, and the Word was God. He was in the beginning with God. All things were made through him, and without him was not any thing made that was made.*[17]

A good hermeneutic will produce the following conclusion: John is writing about Jesus. He's using the reference of "Word" (Greek λόγος, *logos*) to present an important understanding of Jesus' identity, purpose, and work. Jesus is identified as being God, and with God. This is the pre-incarnate Son who is one of the Trinity of God. An essential confession of the Trinity. It also clearly shows that of the three persons of the Trinity (Father, Son, Holy Spirit), it is the Son, or person Jesus Christ, who is the agent of creation.

Now, apply that good hermeneutic to this verse in Genesis.

> *then the LORD God formed the man of dust from the ground and breathed into his nostrils the breath of life, and the man became a living creature.*[18]

When used without any shuffle, the consistent good hermeneutic understands and acknowledges it is The Son, Jesus, who is doing the creative act recorded here. Understanding that Jesus is the Creator helps us appreciate the authority of His statement in Matthew 19.

> *And Pharisees came up to him and tested him by asking, "Is it lawful to divorce one's wife for any cause?" He answered, "Have you not read that he*

---

[17] John 1:1-3
[18] Genesis 2:7

> *who created them from the beginning made them male and female, and said, 'Therefore a man shall leave his father and his mother and hold fast to his wife, and the two shall become one flesh'? So they are no longer two but one flesh. What therefore God has joined together, let not man separate."*[19]

Who is the "he" that Jesus is referring to? Our unshuffled hermeneutic clearly points out that Jesus is referring to the pre-incarnate self. He is the Creator Whom created them male and female with the purpose He designed them to have. His answer to the Pharisees has ultimate authority because He is God. He is the Creator. He was *there!*

Now comes the challenge. So far, it has been easy to keep our hermeneutic without shuffle to show the clear, obvious, understandable presentation of truth in Scripture.

> *Then I saw an angel coming down from heaven, holding in his hand the key to the bottomless pit and a great chain. And he seized the dragon, that ancient serpent, who is the devil and Satan, and bound him for a thousand years, and threw him into the pit, and shut it and sealed it over him, so that he might not deceive the nations any longer, until the thousand years were ended. After that he must be released for a little while. Then I saw thrones, and seated on them were those to whom the authority to judge was committed. Also I saw the souls of those who had been beheaded for the testimony of Jesus and for the word of God, and those who had not worshiped the beast or its image and had not received its mark on their foreheads or their hands. They came to life and*

---

[19] Matthew 19:3-6

> *reigned with Christ for a thousand years. The rest of the dead did not come to life until the thousand years were ended. This is the first resurrection. Blessed and holy is the one who shares in the first resurrection! Over such the second death has no power, but they will be priests of God and of Christ, and they will reign with him for a thousand years.*[20]

How many times are the words "thousand years" used in these verses? Since God always speaks clearly, understandably, purposefully, why would He say a thousand years if He meant something else? If God wanted to say this time interval in which Satan is bound and Christians who have died are resurrected and reign physically with Christ for a time – if God didn't mean a thousand years, why did He say "a thousand"? And why did He repeat it? It is an interesting observation that some young-earth theologians change their hermeneutic when it comes to prophetic passages and eschatology, a study of the "last-things". In particular, regarding the topic of the millennium. Many – not all, but many – turn to a hermeneutic of non-literal, non-real, analogies and types, and spiritualized meaning for last things.

It is as if young-earth theologians are disinterested with eschatology. I have often heard pastors and other church members describe themselves as "pan-millennialists" with a humorous meaning of "it will all pan out at the end". We work hard to apply our hermeneutic and extract the rich truth of the beginning of creation out of Scripture. We diligently sift through the physical evidence in the world around us, conforming our interpretation of that evidence to understand how it also points to a young earth. We are proud of having the correct view of Genesis. It is a good thing that we can state that Genesis is clear and obvious in its meaning. But, when it comes to the end of God's creation, when we are faced with thinking about the final things, we just

---

[20] Revelation 20:1-6

don't care. John MacArthur, Pastor and Teacher with *Grace To You*, noted this same strange correlation.

> *"So, it is really one of the strange ironies of [certain theological systems]. And therefore it's a strange irony in the church today that those who love the doctrine of sovereign election most, ...and who are most unwavering in their devotion to the glory of God, the honor of Christ, the work of the Holy Spirit in regeneration, the veracity and inerrancy of Scripture, those who are usually the most fastidious in Bible interpretation, yes those who are the most careful and intentionally biblical regarding all categories of doctrine, those who see themselves as guardians of biblical truth, those who are passionate to get it right, those who are not content to be wrong at all, and those who most heartily agree on the essential matters of Christian truth so that they labor with all their powers to examine in a Berean fashion every relevant text to discern the true interpretation of all matters of divine revelation are...and there's the main verb in the sentence...are in varying degrees of disinterest in applying their skills to the end of the story and rather content to be in happy if not playful [in] disagreement in regard to the vast biblical data on eschatology as if the end doesn't matter much..."*[21]

---

[21] John MacArthur, "Why Every Calvinist Should Be a Premillennialist, Part 1", Sermon 90-334, March 25, 2007, available online in audio and transcript,
 https://www.gty.org/library/sermons-library/90-334/why-every-calvinist-should-be-a-premillennialist-part-1, accessed September 13, 2017.

CHAPTER 4
WRONG ANSWERS

Allow me to share an interesting irony that occurs in theological circles. There are conservative theologians who view the Genesis record as a real, historical, literal narrative, but turn to the Biblical passages regarding the millennium, like Revelation 20:1-6, and shuffle to an allegoric hermeneutic. They take a stand on reading Genesis, and in particular the creation story, as clear and accurate, insisting on a literal meaning in spite of cultural pressure to the contrary. Yet, depart from the "clear, accurate" interpretation of scripture when it comes to the millennium.

But, isn't some scripture allegorical? Of course *some* is. We find literary devices used throughout scripture. Humor and sarcasm. Similes and allegories. Metaphor and imagery. These are powerful tools in communicating truth.

Here's an important note to having an excellent hermeneutic. We don't have to tell the scriptures when it is using a literary device. Since we've already discovered or understood that God speaks plainly, clearly, and understandably, when He chooses to use a literary device such as a simile or allegory or sarcasm, it will be clear, plain, and understandable that He is doing just that. When allegory is used in scripture, it is clear allegory is used. Scripture is still clear and precise and accurate when using tools of language.

Isn't This Just Allegory?

Allegory as a literary device has a valuable and powerful place in storytelling and in revealing truth. However, it can cause great harm to incorrectly classify a passage as allegorical when it was never meant to be allegory. The intended meaning as well as application of truth can become corrupted to the point of no longer being useful.

This has always been an issue with Scripture. It was a particularly troublesome problem before and during the time of John Calvin. As all

Figure 4 Image of Reformation Wall, or Reformation Monument in Geneva, Switzerland depicting Guillaume Farel, Johannes Calvin, Théodore de Bèze, and John Knox. By Roland Zumbühl: http://www.picswiss.ch/Genf/GE-05-01.html, CC BY-SA 3.0, https://commons.wikimedia.org/w/index.php?curid=632099, accessed June 23, 2015

good defenders of The Faith must do, John Calvin took a strong stand against misidentification of allegory. He understood the dangers of treating a passage as allegorical when it was not. Or, the damage caused by applying an allegorical label to claim hidden meaning. His admonition from a commentary on Corinthians is very instructive and a good warning:

> *"From [the use of allegory] arose a very pernicious error — that of imagining that the perusal of Scripture would be not merely useless, but even injurious, unless it were drawn out into allegories. This error was the source of many evils. For there was not merely a liberty allowed of adulterating the genuine meaning of Scripture, but the more of audacity any one had in this manner of acting, so much the more eminent an interpreter of Scripture was he accounted. Thus many of the ancients recklessly played with the sacred word of God, as if it had been a ball to be tossed to and fro. In consequence of this, too, heretics had it more in their power to trouble the Church; for as it had become general practice to make any passage whatever mean anything that one might choose, there was no frenzy so absurd or monstrous, as not to admit of being brought forward under some pretext of allegory. Even good men themselves were carried headlong, so as to contrive very many mistaken opinions, led astray through a fondness for allegory."*[22]

Young-earth proponents reject the claim the creation account in Genesis and the detailed account of the global flood are allegory, or metaphorical. These accounts are real, historical events. Treating these in any other way than as real history dilutes, if not removes, critical truth. In the same manner, prophecies of the coming Messiah are prophecies concerning real, historic events. Even if a prophecy may contain allegory to describe the real event, that doesn't diminish the real, future-historical reality of the yet-to-be occurrence.

This brings us full-circle to our point. Let's re-ask the question.

---

[22] John Calvin, *Commentary* on 2 Corinthians 3:6, accessed from the Christian Classics Ethereal Library, http://www.ccel.org/ccel/calvin/calcom40.ix.ii.html.

Why Six Days?

Since God speaks, has spoken, clearly, understandably, precisely, accurately, and has said what He intended to say or communicate in accordance with His perfect character and perfect ability, then why did He say that He created in six days followed by a day of rest?

If God had done something other than what He said He did, then why didn't He say that? If we are going to claim science is correct, and humans evolved from a common ancestor over the past four billion years, then why didn't God tell us that is what He did? He is able to say what needed to be said. He is powerful and knowledgeable to communicate so that He can be understood. Although it would be easy and maybe helpful to write another chapter or two and address this question, the answer would come back to this simple conclusion: God cannot lie and He cannot deceive. To do so would make Him not God. It would violate his character as God. Therefore, we should or must conclude He has told us what He did in the creation of the universe. He has told us that He created in six days. And then ceased from creating on the seventh day.

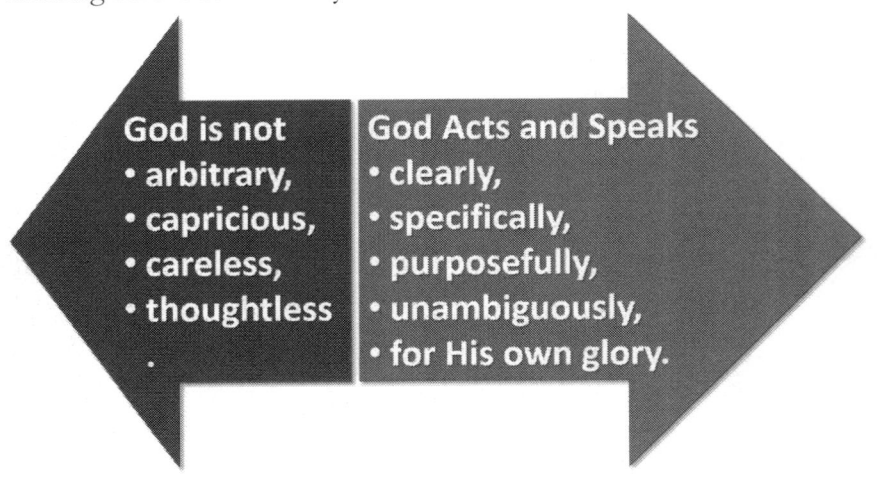

God is not
- arbitrary,
- capricious,
- careless,
- thoughtless

God Acts and Speaks
- clearly,
- specifically,
- purposefully,
- unambiguously,
- for His own glory.

God is not arbitrary, capricious, careless, or thoughtless. He acts and speaks clearly, specifically, purposefully, and unambiguously. And, He does so to bring Himself glory. Human authors will carefully choose words to convey a meaning. Often laboring over the precise words (or single word) in combination with pacing and meter to move the story along. They may add flowery illustrations to help the reader be drawn into the story, or be carried along by the narrative. God does not struggle to find the right word or best word. He doesn't choose a word that another person would question and say "a better way to say this would have been…". His communication is perfect. He doesn't have to add words to make the story flow better, or have just the right pacing. He doesn't have to add illustrations just to bring the reader along.

He knows how to communicate because He is both the perfect communicator and the Creator of communication. He is God. Whenever He speaks, He speaks with extreme purpose. No filler. No words just to make the story longer, or add weight to the story simply by the addition of words. It will revolutionize your view of Scripture if you will read every word with an expectation that every word is placed with *extreme* purpose.

What About Chance?

Of all the theological issues I have grappled with, the Sovereignty of God has been the richest and most challenging. Particularly with regard to what we perceive as random processes.

Our experiences are filled with events that are unpredictable and outcomes that we not only did not foresee, we also lacked any way to foresee or predict. Rolling dice, selecting numbers in a lottery, the pattern of flames over a burning log all appear very random to us. These things, these events, we attribute to chance. Not only do we have no control over them, there doesn't appear to be anything that does. We explain this "uncontrollability" by invoking chaos or chance.

Random events are not the same as unexplainable events. It is common for us to think about them as interchangeable. We need to work hard not to. They are very different.

Why Six Days?

When I was a young adult, the culture was filled with tags and shirts and pictures with a theme of "Stuff Happens".[23] It was a harbinger of the modern meme. It was a cultural adoption of unexplainable chaos wrapped into an attempt of personal irresponsibility. Things happen because they just happen. It's chance. No one is at fault. No one could have changed or controlled some specific event because it was controlled by chance. Random processes had control. Perhaps it is because we are constantly experiencing unexplainable events that we begin to think of chance and random events as not only uncontrollable, but, as having some greater controlling force themselves.

And, just to give it validity, we will assign a scientific principle or law to this randomness. We wrongly think this is what scientists mean by reference to The Second Law of Thermodynamics. You know, that one that says randomness of the universe is increasing. It's a Law of Science that represents what we observe to be true everywhere. Like the First Law that says matter and energy are neither created nor destroyed.

There are several different ways the Second Law of Thermodynamics is expressed or stated. Often, where we apply the definition controls the choice of how it is stated. In general, though, we can use "spontaneous processes in the universe are accompanied by an overall increase in disorder". Or, in an easier to understand form, "spontaneous events more often occur with a decrease in overall order". Consider the example of a nice square stack of bricks. Over time, our experiences has taught us those bricks will not turn into a building by themselves. Instead, over time, that stack of bricks will fall into a disorganized pile of bricks. Their "randomness" will increase.

The problem occurs when our experience leads us to conclude that this randomness is a controlling force. It controls things. Randomness determines the outcome of a coin toss, the result of a dice roll, or the

---

[23] Yes. I know that's not the actual word used. However, there is no need to use the actual word to convey the concept or idea in this case.

pattern of sticks dropped from the hand.[24] Just like that, we move God aside and place the Law of Thermodynamics as higher as a controlling or sovereign power.

It isn't.

The first time I read through the book of Exodus, I encountered many things that never made it into Sunday School lessons or sermons I had heard. For example, the garments of the High Priest were fascinating and filled with meaning. Most fascinating were the *Urim* and *Thummim*. They were at once both fascinating and filled me with confusion.

> And in the breastpiece of judgement you shall put the Urim and the Thummim, and they shall be on Aaron's heart, when he goes in before the LORD. Thus Aaron shall bear the judgement of the people of Israel on his heart before the LORD regularly.[25]

These objects were used to determine the will of God. They were used by Joshua[26] and by King Saul[27] to determine who had hidden something wrongly done. Their purpose was to be used by the High Priest to determine God's will in those situations where there was no other way to know. And, this use is described in every way as appropriate and correct. But, here is the problem. Their use appears to

---

[24] It is important to recognize none of these are truly random. I am using the term "random" in the common way the average person would understand and use the term. A flipped coin is affected by variations in density of the coin, temperature of the metal as it affects the surrounding air, resistance from the air based on surface variations, gravitational force variations, and other forces that also affect the outcome beyond the simple probability. The same is true for most processes we identify as random based on probability, but not physical effects.

[25] Exodus 28:30

[26] Joshua 7:10-25 describes a judgement that had come upon the people of Israel in the defeat at the battle of Ai due to the sin of Achan. Joshua used some type of oracle, or device, that identified the guilty party. Many theologians believes Joshua used the *Urim* and *Thummim*, thought they are not specifically referenced.

[27] 1 Samuel 14:41 records King Saul asking God for judgement to determine who had caused an offense. The use of the *Urim* and *Thummim* is specifically mentioned in the ESV translation.

be controlled by random processes. Like the rolling of dice, these objects are thrown or dropped, and their place, orientation, or position after being dropped used to determine the will of God in a particular situation.

We could assume that God would intervene and cause their outcome to be what was needed so that His will was clear. But, we must then ask, "What do we mean by 'God would intervene'"? Is this a miracle? The suspension of natural processes for the purpose of declaring something particularly important. That kind of miracle?

Except that the processes controlling the *Urim* and *Thummim* are not out of God's control, but in it. To us, the rolling of dice, the flipping of a coin, or the dropping of a stick seem random. God is Sovereign over the processes we view as random. They are not random for Him. Those things we view as chance — the flipping of a coin, the scattering of broken pieces from a dropped and shattered drinking glass — God is Sovereign over these processes. I am not claiming God is directing the movement of every piece of glass shattering on a tile floor from a dropped drinking glass beyond the laws of the universe the glass is dropped in. I am pointing out that God does have control over events we don't acknowledge. Much less understand His control.

We could get derailed from our journey to the answer of "Why Six Days?" by following this truth for much longer. And, what is uncovered in our understanding of the Sovereignty of God is always worth the work. But, for now, let's use this truth to help us understand that God is purposefully giving us information in the six days of creation followed by the seventh day of rest. It didn't just happen that way. God was not limited in the communication nor unable to say something different than what He said. The truth is that God designed the days of creation in just the way He described it happened.

A Few Wrong Answers

In case you aren't in full agreement yet, let's state, for the sake of moving on, "God said what He meant to say". Given this statement, or, in the face of this claim, *why six days followed by a day of rest?*

It was the answer to this question, combined with a study of the claims of evolution, and the reasons for a literal interpretation of Genesis 1-11 that led me to discard my theist-evolution position and take on a young-earth, literal six-day, understanding of Genesis and creation.

The conclusion was that God was using those six days followed by a day of rest to communicate something to His creation. To us. And, for that communication to be understandable, to have meaning, the creation days had to be understood for what they were – six, literal days followed by a seventh real literal day.

I've asked this question of my classes at various universities, and in churches, and in casual conversations. As you may imagine, there are a range of answers. Seldom are they the answer I arrived at. Instead, the answers generally fall into several common and clearly wrong groups.

One common wrong answer is, "God didn't have the ability to do it all at once. He had to 'pace' Himself." We must immediately recognize this answer is not based on the God revealed in Scripture and His creation. The god of this answer is not all-powerful. A limited god. This god is so limited we must ask why we think this god is a god at all? This is a man-sized god. A god based on the image, or imagination, of man. More man-like than God-like. This is a man-sized god more than a God-sized God. I encourage anyone that would answer this way to abandon that false god and come worship the true and living God of creation. Pacing due to limitation isn't the answer. Not in any form.

Another common wrong answer is, "God knew that creation had to be built in sequence, just as building a house requires a sequence of steps. You have to lay the foundation, then add floors, build walls, only then can you add the plumbing and electrical wiring, after which you can add the internal wall sheeting, ..." This also reflects a small-god view of the creator. Another answer based on a "man-sized-god" image of God. A God-sized God could place the electrical wiring in place first and then put up the walls. A God-sized Creator could place the shingles first and then much later add the foundation. That's what the concept of God is. Omnipotent. He can do anything He wants to do. In fact, a God-sized God could have created the whole thing in one step, everything at once, without need of a sequence. God isn't constrained by a sequence of events. The need for sequence isn't the answer.

Then, there is the, "God knew man would need a rest. That man should only work in six-day cycles followed by a time of rest to recuperate and prepare for the next six-day cycle of work." At least three problems with this. First, this attempt to use the omniscience of God presupposes that God could not create man to need only one day of rest out of 8 days of work, or 80 days of work, or 800 days of work. Second, it places God in a subordinate role to the need of the week. God knew the week would have a requirement over man, so, God created the week to get around this requirement. Wrong. Finally, this answer confuses the meaning and understanding of the word "rest", and the purpose of the Sabbath. God could have created man to not need physical rest at all. The creation of the seventh day, or the designation of the seventh day as a "Day of Rest" is not a reflection of the need to physically recuperate or the statement of man's physiological need for a time for his physical body to regenerate an ability to work. Recuperation isn't the answer.

There are other answers which are just as wrong. And, there are answers that are "more" wrong. We should take the time to consider at least one of these because it may help us avoid other wrong answers when they occur.

This is any answer based on God picking a number because there was something special and intrinsic in the number itself. It is the "God's favorite number is seven" answer. Problem is, God doesn't have "favorite" numbers. Humans do. Mankind does. God created numbers and math and the relationships of quantities as well as the concept of quantity. He is the Creator of the very thing we are placing equal to Him. God is not a man. Men are not God. God is God. Any use God has for numbers is to reveal. God uses the numbers He created for the purpose of revealing His Glory to us.

One final wrong answer to set us up for a conclusion. This is any answer that claims God is so far above us that even though He wants us to know something, we are unable to understand. It is the answer that compares the problem of God speaking to us with humans attempting to communicate with ants. The difference is too great, is the claim. Yet, God is still God. Remember? "All knowing" means He knows how to say exactly what needs to be said in exactly the correct way so that humans can receive exactly what He wants to communicate. God can not only speak in a way that humans can understand, He can speak in a way that ants can understand. He's God. The ability to speak to His creation goes with the title.

Why Six Days?

The Wrong Answers
- God ~~was~~ weak and needed to "pace" Himself
- God knew that He ~~had~~ to follow a sequence of creation
- God ~~had~~ to create the "week" because He knew we would need a "day of rest"
- God ~~likes~~ the number seven

Why Six Days?

CHAPTER 5
APPLYING THE NON-SHUFFLING, REALLY GOOD HERMENEUTIC

If you've been in church for any length of time, you are probably familiar with the story of Jesus "cleaning" the temple. He didn't use cleanser and a broom. It wasn't that kind of cleaning. He used a whip. Rather startling in our view of the loving, gentle teacher. He used a whip to drive out the self-serving, self-promoting, self-enriching. The temple was filthy with the dirt of humans corrupting the role and purpose God had established for the temple. It cried out to be cleaned and the Creator of the Universe in human form obliged. I used a bit of a literary device there. See?

There is a part of this story that makes it more interesting. Something contained in the story that makes the meaning compelling. It is more startling than the story that He cleaned the temple. That "something" is *when* He cleaned the temple. Jesus could have gone into the temple any day the money changers and sacrificial animal sellers where there. Or, on any given Sabbath – and there were several ordinary as well as special sabbaths every year to choose from. Yet, in this cleansing of the temple, Jesus purposefully chose to do this on one of the Feast celebration days.

There are seven Feast days He could have chosen from. Yet, He purposefully, intentionally chose to clean the Temple on the Feast of Passover. This was a very high Sabbath. A Sabbath of Sabbaths. It was like Christmas and Easter and Super Bowl Sunday all wrapped into one. Instead of taking care of business when it wouldn't have caused such a stir and confusion, Jesus picked this extraordinary day.

Figure 5 "Cleansing the Temple", woodcut for "The Bible in Pictures", 1860. Julius Schnorr von Carolsfeld. Public domain.

Why? That's the type of question we must ask. And, we must answer correctly. Our modern minds want to offer a gentle correction posed in the form of an unassuming question in our attempt to be inclusive and tolerant. Surely Jesus could have caused less of an uproar, less of interruption to the worshippers (after all, they weren't doing anything

Applying the Non-Shuffling, Really Good Hermeneutic

wrong), less of a huge problem if He had selected another day. But, He didn't. Surely, if He had just followed Matthew 18[28], this would have avoided any public humiliation of the merchants and money-changers.

Yet, He chose this Sabbath that was also the Feast of Passover. In fact, His choosing of it should be properly understood as *ordained it*. Jesus wasn't just lucky that a Feast of Passover and a seventh day of the week occurred on the same day in this year in which He was an adult and in Jerusalem and on the face of the earth instead of still in Heaven with the Father and Holy Spirit. Are you starting to see the incredible purpose and intentionality of His cleaning the Temple on this Feast of Passover?

The Jewish leaders were upset and clearly confused. And offended. They asked Jesus to justify what He was doing. They asked for a reason. Actually, they demanded that Jesus give a justification for what He was doing. They framed their offense in a demand. "How dare He do this? What possible justification could He offer for interrupting the Temple worship on this day?" Jesus' answer was as purposeful and intentional as the choice of day for cleaning out the temple.

If you think it was convenient or accidental or coincidental that Jesus cleansed the temple and made this very specific and clear answer on the Passover, then you aren't thinking about God as God. Take a moment and read His answer to the Pharisees' demand.

> *So the Jews* said to him, "What sign do you show us for doing these things?" Jesus answered them, "Destroy this temple, and in three days I will raise it up."[29]

Using a consistent and good hermeneutic, we understand that Jesus meant three days. Three understandable periods of time any person

---

[28] Matthew 18:15-20 is an important teaching of Jesus on the proper manner of dealing with an sinning brother or sister in Christ. It is often used as a hammer against someone attempting to publicly correct a person guilty of a public sin, where, although this teaching is still important, the public part of the sin must still be addressed.
[29] John 2:18-19

would agree constitute the meaning of "day". It is easy in this passage to pull out the right meaning and understand what Jesus was prophesying with His actions and words, because the Gospel writer, John, filled in that information.

> *The Jews then said, "It has taken forty-six years to build this temple, and will you raise it up in three days?" But he was speaking about the temple of his body. When therefore he was raised from the dead, his disciples remembered that he had said this, and they believed the Scripture and the word that Jesus had spoken.[30]*

The proper, non-shifting hermeneutic provides the correct understanding of scripture with an incredible revelation of information about God and His redemptive work. Do you recall when Jesus was crucified? By "when", I mean "what day"? We know, the specific day of the Jewish calendar year. It was on the Feast of the Passover, as seen in John 19:31[31]. Yep. And, when did He rise from being dead? Three days later. One of the reasons Jesus chose to clean the Temple on the Feast of the Passover was this prophetic moment. He knew the corruption of the Temple from its design and purpose, and those who had corrupted it. He knew of the corruption of worship of God that had been introduced by the legalistic teachings and extra-Biblical requirements introduced by the Jewish leadership. He knew that what they had done was impacting the message of the Gospel that underlay every aspect of the Old Testament sacrifice system. The Feast of Passover celebrated the deliverance of the Jewish people from their slavery under the Egyptian empire. This deliverance was a type and foreshadowing of the ultimate deliverance from the slavery to the sin

---

[30] John 2:20-22
[31] "Since it was the day of Preparation, and so that the bodies would not remain on the cross on the Sabbath (for that Sabbath was a high day), the Jews asked Pilate that their legs might be broken and that they might be taken away." John 19:31

Applying the Non-Shuffling, Really Good Hermeneutic

empire all humans are under. The Passover required the use of a perfect lamb that was killed, and whose blood was used as a sign of accepting the promise of deliverance from judgement.

Jesus knew what the Pharisees would ask. His answer pointed them back to their need for a perfect sacrifice to pay for their sins. Just as they had to kill the innocent lamb and offered it as payment for their sin, so they would kill the Lamb of God Who would then become the lamb sacrifice offered as final and complete payment for their sin. So, did Jesus' answer mean three days? Three real, literal, understandable days? Of course. And three days after He died on a cross on the Feast of Passover, paying the final and complete and perfect price for sin, after three days, He arose from the dead. Proving forever that He was Who He said He was and affirming the forgiveness of sin He had purchased for us.

Perhaps you've observed that my example is far more than just illustrating a non-shifting hermeneutic. If so, you have made a good observation. If not, you have now.

Let's look at another example of how not shifting our hermeneutic can also help point to the answer of "Why Six Days?"

Jesus and His disciples were walking through a grain field on the Sabbath and became hungry. So, the disciples pulled off the heads of grain in their hands, rubbed the grain to remove the husk, blew away the chaff, and were eating the grain. The Pharisees accused them of doing work that was not lawful on the Sabbath. After all, they were harvesting and processing the wheat. This was work. Jesus' response referred to the account of David eating bread set aside in the Temple, and Priests doing their priestly service on the Sabbath as examples that work is done on the Sabbath and it wasn't against God's law. Once again Jesus is confronting the Pharisees legalistic additions to God's law, showing them they had attempted to add more to God's law, making it into something that it wasn't meant to be. The two examples Jesus used showed that the Sabbath wasn't holy because it contained something special in or of itself by simply being "the Sabbath". What made the Sabbath important wasn't intrinsic to the actual day. What made the Sabbath important was something else. We might note, something greater.

And then Jesus followed his correction of their thinking with a rather amazing claim.

> I tell you, something greater than the temple is here. And if you had known what this means, 'I desire mercy, and not sacrifice,' you would not have condemned the guiltless. For the Son of Man is lord of the Sabbath."[32]

Is Jesus allegorically Lord of the Sabbath, or is He really, physically, specifically Lord of the Sabbath? He is the real, literal, Lord of the Sabbath. The claim that Jesus makes is clear and unambiguous. It doesn't require secret or special knowledge to understand this claim.

Is Jesus metaphorically Lord of the Sabbath? No. Jesus did not say, "For the Son of Man is like the Lord of the Sabbath." He is the real, literal Lord of the Sabbath.

---

[32] Matthew 12:6-8

CHAPTER 6
GOD EXPECTS HIS PEOPLE TO UNDERSTAND

Throughout the New Testament Gospels, Jesus often answers questions by stating, "Have you not read…" Our modern minds, constrained with unacknowledged cultural filters, comprehend this as nothing more than a bridge to the answer. It's a gentle transition from question to answer. It is, however, more than that. It is a rebuke. Jesus knew the person asking the question. Often someone from the elite in society. Those who were at the pinnacle of their education. And, in the Jewish culture, that education required extensive study of what we know as the Old Testament. Particularly the books of the Law (Genesis, Exodus, Leviticus, Numbers, and Deuteronomy) along with the historical books of the accounts under the Judges and Kings. To be a Pharisee or Scribe required demonstration of knowledge in these areas. So, when Jesus began an answer by stating (not asking, stating) "Have you not read…", it was a rebuke. They read and studied. Yet, the question posed to the Lord was characterized as if it was asked by someone who had never even read the very scripture they claimed expertise in.

God expects His people to understand.

Why Six Days?

This is another critical piece of Biblical interpretative skill. More importantly, it is a critically important Biblical living skill. It can be viewed as having two essential parts. The first is that God's Word is understandable. This is referred to as the perspicuity of Scripture. Here's one of those words many Christians are not familiar with. I believe it should be a common tool in every Christian's toolbox.

Larry Pettegrew, Professor of Theology at the Master's Seminary, describes perspicuity of scripture as, "Scripture is clear enough for the simplest person to live by... deep enough for readers of the highest intellectual ability... clear in its essential matters."[33] Scripture is understandable to the extent necessary for each person to comprehend what they need to know to fully live in accordance with God's Word.

The second essential part is that we are responsible to understand to the limit of our ability to understand. Let's simply acknowledge that is the responsibility of the individual.

The foundation of this understanding that Scripture is understandable is based in a God Who reveals Himself. He doesn't give us information that is designed to hide or confuse knowledge. God's revelation is given in a way to be understandable. Therefore, His Word, the Bible, is understandable.

God both intends for us to understand what He reveals to us and expects Christians to understand what He reveals. He doesn't give us revelation simply to make Himself look mysterious or beyond our comprehension. He is all of those, and doesn't need to prove it.

God's desire to be understood, and for His people to understand what He gives us is woven throughout scripture. The combination of understanding and prophecy is included in those. For example, consider this expectation of understanding in the prophecy given to Daniel.

---

[33] Larry Pettegrew, "The Perspicuity of Scripture", *The Master's Seminary Journal*, 15/2 (Fall 2004), p. 214. Available online at
https://www.monergism.com/thethreshold/sdg/The%20Perspicuity%20of%20Scripture%20by%20Gerry%20Breshears.pdf.

God Expects His People to Understand

> *Know therefore and understand, that from the going forth of the commandment to restore and to build Jerusalem unto the Messiah the Prince shall be seven weeks, and threescore and two weeks: the street shall be built again, and the wall, even in troublous times.*[34]

The angel giving this prophecy to Daniel commanded him to understand. How could the angel give this command if there was no expectation that Daniel *could* understand? God knew Daniel had the capability to understand. Even though the prophecy describes things that, at the time it was given, had not come to pass. Even though the prophecy described future events that Daniel could not understand as we can, he still understood. The various interpretations associated with this prophecy are not the result of it being too difficult to understand. Those often conflicting explanations are from using a hermeneutic that attempts to fit the events into a needed narrative, instead of allowing the prophecy impact our narrative. Using an eisegesis (reading into the prophecy a meaning) instead of an exegesis (pulling our an existing meaning from the prophecy).

However, the meaning was very clear to those prior to the fulfillment. It is very clear to us following it's fulfillment. This prophecy was exactly fulfilled. Precisely fulfilled by a God Who is perfect, unchanging, able to communicate, able to tell us what He wants us to know. And, He calls us to understand. God's Word does not contain revelation that cannot be understood. It contains meaning, words, ideas, concepts that are meant to be understood. And, they are clear.

This prophecy clearly tells us that from the time of a command given to rebuild Jerusalem until the arrival of the Messiah would be a very specific period of time. God didn't give Daniel this very specific revelation for the sake of confusing him or us. He gave the revelation so that Daniel and we could know and understand. If we are confused

---

[34] Daniel 9:25 KJV

by the communication, then the idea, the concept, the purpose of the communication is lost. God doesn't attempt to show us how great He is by showing us how easy we are to confuse. God shows His greatness by clear communication that is understandable.

Jesus often called on people to understand and then act on that understanding. It is true that He spoke in parables for the sake of making somethings only clear to those He had chosen to understand. But, they were still expected to understand.

Jesus, also, expected that what He said to be understood. This is particularly clear in the Parable of the Sower.[35] Jesus used these word, "He who has ears to hear, let him hear." Often, I have heard people interpret this as a statement of selective messaging. That only certain people had ears to hear this. That is true and clear in all three Gospels. Jesus states that He spoke in parables so that those who were in rebellion to the Word of God would not understand. But, He also stated that for those who He intended to receive the message, they were also intended to be able to hear it. They had ears. Therefore, they should hear. And, in hearing, understand. He said, "To you it has been given to know the secrets of the kingdom of God."[36] God expects the intended recipients of His revelation to know, comprehend, understand that revelation.

This call to understand is repeated in The Revelation as each of the seven churches are addressed by Jesus. John records the words of Jesus as He speaks very specific instruction to each of these churches.

> *He who has an ear, let him hear what the Spirit says to the churches.'*[37]

---

[35] This is found in the Gospels of Matthew (13:1-23) as well as Mark (4:1-20) and Luke (8:4-15).
[36] Luke 8:10, Matthew 13:11
[37] Revelation 2:29

It is clear they are intended to not just receive the instruction. They are to understand. And, in understanding, to act. God intends for us to know and understand.

Why six days followed by a day of rest? There must be knowable meaning.

Why Six Days?

CHAPTER 7
THE PATTERN

You may wish to argue that it's only in this passage from Genesis 1 and 2 that we find this pattern of six followed by a seventh. So, what's the big deal? Only this. Just because you haven't seen the pattern anywhere else doesn't mean it isn't there. And, just because you may think it isn't a "big deal" is not the same as it not being a big deal. What if it is a big deal to God? If it is important enough to Him to tell us about this, shouldn't it become or be important to us?

Since God doesn't act randomly or without purpose, there must be some reason God created in six days, and then carefully worked to tell us what He has done. After all, He is careful in many other places to reveal Himself through what He has done or is doing. Why not in the six days followed by a seventh day of rest, also?

Along the Appalachian Mountains that run from Georgia to Maine in the United States is a famous hiking trail. It is famous for its 2,190 mile length and the challenge it offers to individuals to hike the trail from one end to the other. An accomplishment with motivation similar to summiting Mt. Everest (or any other similar challenge). In addition to the accomplishment, the experience and views along the journey are not repeatable in any other experience.

Along the southern end of that mountain range is another trail for cars. The Blue-Ridge Parkway. Like the hiking trail, it is designed for the journey instead of the destination. It is a winding and narrow road, with various "turn-offs" to stop and take in the breath-taking scenery and vistas. It is a journey designed for a slower pace that allows the traveler to experience the countryside. The journey is the goal.

Considering the pattern of "six followed by a seventh" is a similar journey. We need to appreciate the designer of the Blue-Ridge Parkway for adding the turn-offs. Taking the time to stop and take in the incredible vistas. God placed "turn-offs" in our lives, and in His Word, so that we can see there is much along the road. The journey has a destination. And, there are places along the way that are designed to help us understand that destination.

Our first stop to take in the view is the names of the days of the week.

The names for the days of the week may at first appear unimaginative and boring. Like driving on an interstate. We use them to get to the destination without care for what may be "underneath". Our goal is the end. The weekend. Our leisure time. Along the way, we don't have time to consider the names of each day. Or, the meaning in those names. However, the stop to take in the view has value.

The Hebrew names, in comparison to the English names, appear unimaginative and boring. The first day of the week is called *Yom Rishon*, meaning "Day One". The second day corresponding to the English "Monday" is, *Yom Sheni*, or "Second Day". Before you intellectually toss this aside, pause as you would if driving up a mountain road and stopping at a turn-off and see if there is something worth taking in. Do these names offer something deeper than their English counterparts? Are the Hebrew names of each day of the week "pointing" to something?

English weekday names have meaning, also. They are derived from old English and deeper Latin names, and associated with the gods of pagan pantheism. The old English names reflected gods in the pantheism of the "Northland" including Germanic and Norse gods. These were related by Latin names to gods in the Roman and older religions.

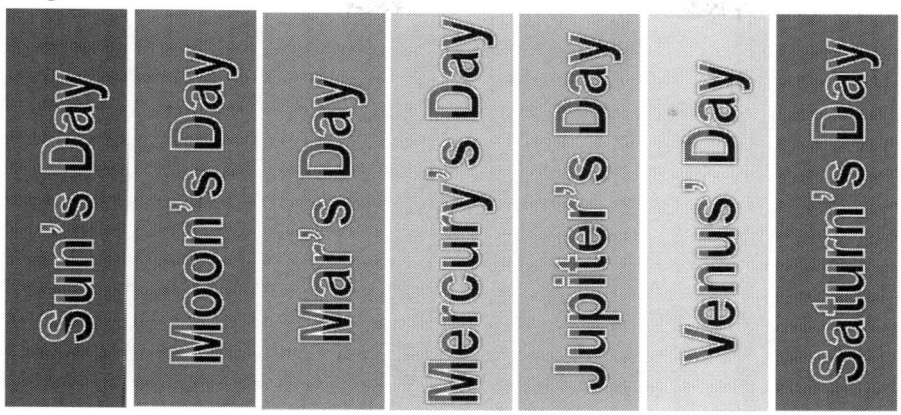

| Sun's Day | Moon's Day | Mar's Day | Mercury's Day | Jupiter's Day | Venus' Day | Saturn's Day |

In contrast to celebrating pagan gods, the Hebrew names celebrate the creation week. And, they do so every week of every month of every year since creation. Each day is a reminder back to the creation itself. Instead of simple and unimaginative, using these names for each day confesses the creation event. "First Day", "Second Day"…and then the seventh. Not named "Seventh Day". But, *Yom Shabbat,* which means "Rest Day" in honor and observance of the Day of Creation in which God "rested".

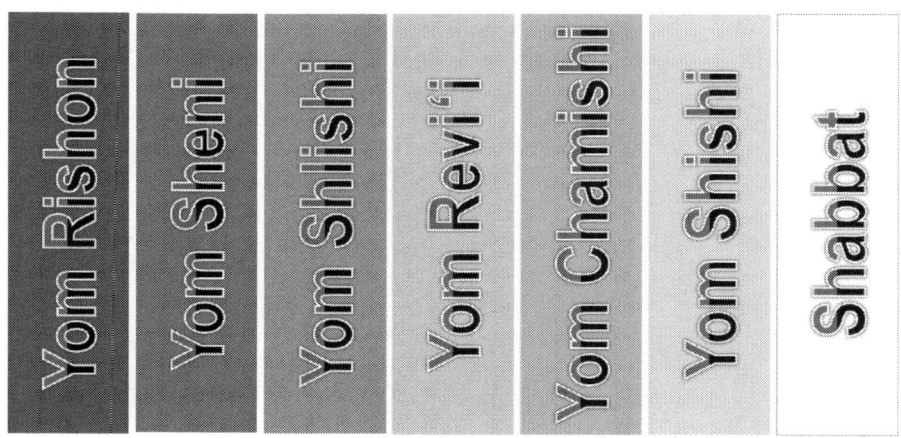

| Yom Rishon | Yom Sheni | Yom Shlishi | Yom Revi'i | Yom Chamishi | Yom Shishi | Shabbat |

What an incredible contrast in worship this is to what we have adopted as normal and acceptable for the English names. Perhaps we've lost something. What if, in our loss of using these proper names for the days of the week, names that confess the creator on a daily/weekly basis, and point back to the creation week as a reminder; what if we have lost a valuable tool? It is possible the lessons in the names of the days as a confession of creation contains utility for today. Perhaps, even, for the Gospel.

To properly answer the question of "Why six days?", we need to first understand the importance of the six-day period followed by a seventh day of rest. Is Genesis the only place we find God using this sequence of six followed by a seventh?

It's in The Ten Commandments

Our second turn-off along this road is to stop and consider the Decalogue, or Ten Commandments.

Most of us would not be comfortable ranking the Ten Commandments in order of importance. Even though we might agree there is a hierarchy in the commandments, it makes us a bit nervous to identify it. This fear is well-founded. We are not the authors. And, the commands themselves do not have a hierarchy associated with them that is easy to identify. Still, we would give greater importance to those commandments which are clearly linked to the person of God. Like the First Command, "Have no other gods before Me." In whatever ranking of commandments we would have, near the top of most of those would be the command to keep or honor the Sabbath day.

> "Remember the Sabbath day, to keep it holy. Six days you shall labor, and do all your work, but the seventh day is a Sabbath to the LORD your God. On it you shall not do any work, you, or your son, or your daughter, your male servant, or your female servant, or your livestock, or the sojourner who is within your gates.

The Pattern

> *For in six days the LORD made heaven and earth, the sea, and all that is in them, and rested on the seventh day. Therefore the LORD blessed the Sabbath day and made it holy.* [38]

And here we have to mark something different. Each of the Ten Commandments could stand by themselves. But, God incorporated illuminating statements for Commandments 2, 4, and 5. Although verse 2 of Exodus 20 could be taken as a general introduction to all Ten Commands, it gives particular clarity to the first. When God states, "I Am the Lord your God", and then command that we only worship Him, it adds emphasis and clarity to the command. There is only one God. He is the same God Who delivered you from bondage. Since there is only one God, one real God, He should be worshipped singly, only, without dilution.

The next command similarly adds clarification: Worship God without attempting to make an image of God. Making any image would corrupt the correct worship of God. He tells us that He is jealous with regard to our worship of Him. Each of these commands are clearly related to the person of God and our worship of Him.

Just as the fourth commandment is. The command to honor a specific day of the week.

Here is a particularly interesting Commandment. This Commandment is one with the "extra" information. The illuminating statements. Or, if you will, an "anchor". This commandment to honor the Sabbath contains an anchor that fixes the reason for the Commandment within God's revelation of Himself. And, therefore, in His redemptive plan. It also serves as a reference point to guard against the tendency we humans have to make our obedience a simple legalistic action. A reminder that this, too, is related to the Person and Work of God and our proper worship of Him. Therefore, God gives the purpose

---

[38] Exodus 20:8-11

and reason. Work six days celebrates the creation week. Resting on the seventh day – the Sabbath day – celebrates and honors the day God rested. An anchor of meaning that helps us know *why*.

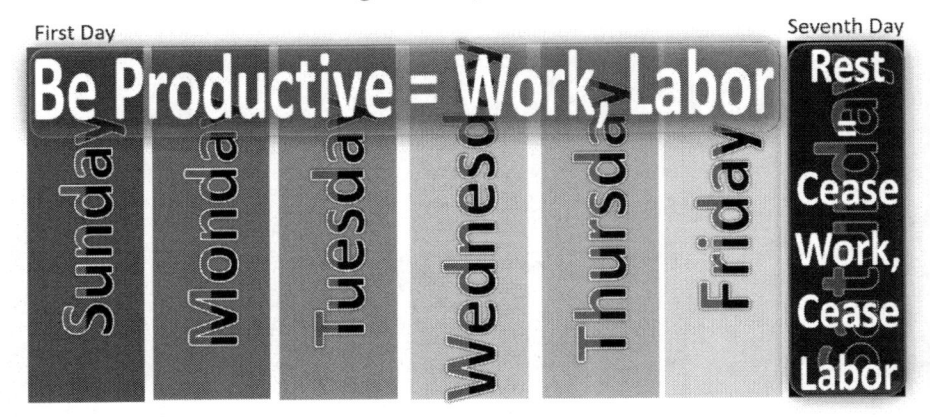

First Day — Be Productive = Work, Labor — Sunday, Monday, Tuesday, Wednesday, Thursday, Friday | **Seventh Day** — Rest, Cease Work, Cease Labor (Saturday)

Therefore, the first two layers of meaning are that God has established a set-apart (holy) day for particular worship. And, He has linked that specific day of worship to the creation week. Specifically, the seventh day of the creation week. The six other days of the week are also days of worship in that all we do on every day is an act of confession and obedience. God gave us work to do as a gift from Him. In doing our work, we acknowledge that gift and the source. We are called to "work as unto the Lord"[39] – to do every work as belonging to Him. Though we serve earthly masters, the capacity to do work, whether it is intellectual or physical, is from God. He gave both the ability (minds, bodies, strength) to complete the work and He gave the work itself. We worship Him every day of the week. Those days are also linked to the creation week when God did the work of creating. Our work on those days should also be a confession that He created all that is. And then we cease on one day as He did to acknowledge that He is Sovereign over all, and that He stopped working on the seventh day.

---

[39] Whatever you do, work heartily, as for the Lord and not for men, knowing that from the Lord you will receive the inheritance as your reward. You are serving the Lord Christ. Colossians 3:23-24

The week that our modern world uses as the cycle for business, commerce, culture is a constant reflection of the six days of creation followed by the day of rest that God established in the first week.

It is Much More than The Ten Commandments

The Pattern in the Flood of Noah

After the creation week, the first place historically we find this pattern of six days followed by the seventh is recorded in the flood account. It is in the story of "Noah's" flood.

In Genesis chapters six through eight, we find an amazing amount of information about the flood. Details of precise times, instructions, and historical events. The key to this treasure-house of information is understanding that God choose to preserve these details of the events. Remember that God doesn't act maliciously, arbitrarily, or purposelessly. He acts with extreme purpose and intent. Therefore, these details have been recorded for the Glory of God and for our benefit.

> *"Then the LORD said to Noah, "Go into the ark, you and all your household, …. For in seven days I will send rain on the earth forty days and forty nights, and every living thing that I have made I will blot out from the face of the ground."*[40]

God chose to command Noah to enter the ark seven days before the flood commenced. He could have selected any number – four days, ten days, two – but, He chose seven. Noah and his family, and all the animals, spent the last week of the pre-flood world on the ark. We can speculate using informed intellect as to what may have been accomplished during this time, and the usefulness of this pre-flood time on the ark. Perhaps Noah and his family finalized their daily work

---

[40] Exert from Genesis 7:1-4

routines of caring for themselves and for the animals before being cut-off from any resources they could have in the pre-flood time. Perhaps this was a final statement to the condemned world which demonstrated the provision of God's saving grace which they had rejected.

Noah and his family were facing an unknown yet known cataclysmic event. They knew what God had told Noah. God was going to completely destroy all air-breathing life on the face of the whole earth. Perhaps unable to comprehend the totality of the event, they knew it *was* coming. And, that it was going to be horrible. This week, this seven-day period, if it had been something they practiced all their lives, provided comfort of familiarity in their new surroundings. It is possible they had already practiced this pattern of working six days and resting on the seventh. It was routine for them. Now, it was a time just before the judgement of the flood that gave them some comfort. It gave them confidence.

Just as the week had a start and a finish, and was then followed by the next week, this week on the ark spoke a message to them of comfort that God had ordained the passage of weeks. This coming judgement would start and it would finish, and then be followed by the ordained time that came after. The week started and finished. The flood would start and it would finish.

Again, it is reasonable to conclude Noah was following God-given instruction in this cycle of a seven-day week. How God gave that pattern to the pre-flood, pre-Ten-Commandment world, we don't know. However, it is reasonable to conclude that Noah and other antediluvian people observed a seven day week because they knew God created all that is in six days and rested on the seventh.

The pattern occurs again as the flood concludes. As the flood waters began to recede from the land, we read that Noah performed a series of tests to determine what was occurring outside the ark.

> *And the waters continued to abate until the tenth month; in the tenth month, on the first day of the*

The Pattern

> *month, the tops of the mountains were seen. At the end of forty days Noah opened the window of the ark that he had made and sent forth a raven. It went to and fro until the waters were dried up from the earth. Then he sent forth a dove from him, to see if the waters had subsided from the face of the ground. But the dove found no place to set her foot, and she returned to him to the ark, for the waters were still on the face of the whole earth. So he put out his hand and took her and brought her into the ark with him.*[41]

Theologians have attempted to explain Noah's selection of these two types of birds. First the raven and then the dove. Perhaps ravens are more willing to get their feet wet than doves. A reasonable understanding uses the known eating habits of both bird types. Ravens are known to be omnivorous and opportunistic in their feeding, while pigeons are known to prefer seeds and fruits. As the water receded from the land, we can speculate the presence of food in the form of carrion or plant matter the raven would be able to eat. However, it would take time for a plant to begin growing and produce something that would attract the pigeon. That new growth from the pigeon is what Noah recognized as indicating the earth's surface could support the animals in the ark.

There is a clear description of the timing of the bird's release. And, there is purpose is Noah's timing in releasing the birds.

> *He waited another seven days, and again he sent forth the dove out of the ark. And the dove came back to him in the evening, and behold, in her mouth was a freshly plucked olive leaf. So Noah knew that the waters had subsided from the earth. Then he waited*

---
[41] Genesis 8:5-9

Why Six Days?

another seven days and sent forth the dove, and she did not return to him anymore.[42]

Figure 6 The pattern in Noah releasing birds from the ark. Three separate seven-day cycles.

There are three sets of seven days. The first is referenced by the statements, "he waited another seven days". That means within the first release was a seven-day cycle. And then the second release of birds, and then a third time after a third period of seven days, Noah released the dove for the final time. This time, the dove did not return.

The rational conclusion is Noah was already following this pattern of a seven-day week. He was already following a pattern of Sabbath observation. We are not given any details related to this observation. But, we are given details to indicate Noah was following some type of seven-day cycle. A cycle that was both present and observed. It is also obvious that Noah brought this from the pre-flood world. There is no reason for the flood to have caused this seven-day cycle. Therefore, it was a practice to observe this seven-day cycle even before the flood.

---

[42] Genesis 8:10-12

Between Deliverance from Egypt and the Giving of the Law

We encounter another occurrence of the seven-day cycle while the people of Israel are in the wilderness after their miraculous release from captivity in Egypt.[43] When we consider the context of God's sovereignty in allowing the captivity to occur, and the means of deliverance with the miracles that point to the coming Messiah, there is an abundant and rich wealth of revelation in this story. Perhaps you recall the story as the people of Israel left Egypt and crossed the Red Sea.[44] They walked on dry land across the sea floor. They were immediately delivered from Pharaoh's army which were drowned in the sea, after which the nation of Israel found themselves in a barren land. A nation of thousands with no established agriculture, no on-going food production. Whatever food they brought out of Egypt was consumed in a short time. They became hungry.

The Exodus account isn't just about the great things God did in delivering the Israelites from bondage in Egypt. God chose to also include those things we may not want to think about. Those things that included these same people acting in an ungrateful way to the very God who had delivered them from slavery. The people became hungry. They focused on their inability to provide food for themselves. Instead of answering their own concern with trust in God, they chose to sin, and grumbled, complaining that God had allowed them to come into the wilderness to die of hunger. God acted by providing a food, called "manna".[45] The provision of the manna is another miraculous event that foretells of God's provision of grace and life in the coming Messiah.

---

[43] The full story is found in Exodus 3 – 13.
[44] Exodus 14
[45] Exodus 16:1-36. The name for the food, "manna" means "what is it?" A fascinating name with meaning that may be difficult for the modern or post-modern mind to appreciate. The people would know any natural substance that was a common food source. Apparently, this wasn't common. But, it was food. What is it?

Woven into this miracle is the pattern of sabbath observation. God instructed the people to gather every day only what they could use for each person that day. He also instructed them that on the sixth day they were to gather twice as much, for the next day there would be no manna. And, they should not go out on that seventh day to gather it. They were to rest. The seventh day was identified by the title of a sabbath (Exodus 16:29).

In our modern lives, we may think this idea of a sabbath was something established by God when He gave the Ten Commandments. However, there is clear evidence it existed and was observed before the visit to Mt. Sinai. And, very likely, was a celebration and confession of God's creative act of six days followed by a day of rest.

Figure 7 The Pattern of Gathering Manna. Image is a portion of Bernardino Luini, *The Gathering of the Manna*, painted between 1520-1523. Image accessed from the Web Gallery of Art,

CHAPTER 8
THE PATTERN EMPHASIZED

Are we making too much of this? That's an important question. And, one we should ask often, and properly answer. Just as important is the mirror-image question to this one: Are we making too little of this? Have we dismissed as not important something that is important?

When I answer these paired questions, one very helpful criteria is to simply look for how much of God's Word is attributed to the issue. Although this is not by itself a final determination of importance, it is a strong indicator. When I am teaching, and I want to make sure the students perceive that something I am teaching is important, I will repeat it. All of us do this. Speaking to our children, our spouses, our friends – if we have something we want to make sure they hear us, we emphasize by repetition. We repeat ourselves for emphasis. Just like that.

So, when God repeats Himself, perhaps we should slow down for a closer look. We should see what it is He believes is important enough that He repeats it. And after we see that He has repeated something for emphasis, we should then take the time to find out what it is God is wanting us to know.

This pattern of six followed by a distinct but related seventh is repeated. It was revealed in the creation week, repeated in the Ten Commandments, and apparently practiced by individual before the flood and before the Ten Commandments were given. It is also repeated in the Levitical laws given to the nation of Israel.

The Sabbath Year

After laying the foundation of this pattern of six followed by a seventh by creating the week and making it both a constant act of worship and constant act of confession of creation, God then emphasizes this pattern. This emphasis of six items followed by a seventh is layered, one on top of another. There are layers of pattern. On top of the weekly cycle of six days followed by the seventh day, God establishes a pattern of years that is identical to the pattern of days.

Figure 8 The Sabbath cycle emphasized in a period of seven years.

God established and commanded the observance of six years of harvest followed by a seventh year of rest – a Sabbath Year.

> "For six years you shall sow your land and gather in its yield, but the seventh year you shall let it rest and lie fallow, that the poor of your people may eat; and what they leave the beasts of the field may eat. You

The Pattern Emphasized

shall do likewise with your vineyard, and with your olive orchard.[46]

Just as before, to understand the meaning God intends, if we desire to know the purpose, we must remind ourselves that God is not capricious, or arbitrary. He acts with extreme purpose.

Note that God did not say that during the seventh year, the Sabbath year, there would be no fruit. He would still provide fruit for the poor and for the animals. The ground would still produce harvest. The difference was in the work. God's people were not allowed to work or strive. They had to cease from striving to produce for themselves out of God's common providence. God would produce. He would provide. In fact, in Leviticus 25[47], God makes it clear He would provide sufficient produce during the sixth year for all their needs during the following Sabbath year, as well as the year after that (the eighth year). In the sixth year, God would provide sufficient for needs of the sixth year, the seventh year (when the people could not harvest), and the next year when they would have normally relied on the harvest from the seventh year to keep them until the harvest of the first year.

God provided. It was His provision the people would have to rely on. He was the source of what they would normally need to rely on themselves to obtain. The could cease from work. They had to cease from work. Every harvest was based in God's provision. But, in the seventh year, they were particularly dependent on God's provision, which was His work, for their salvation.

---

[46] Exodus 23:10-11

[47] "And if you say, 'What shall we eat in the seventh year, if we may not sow or gather in our crop?' I will command my blessing on you in the sixth year, so that it will produce a crop sufficient for three years. When you sow in the eighth year, you will be eating some of the old crop; you shall eat the old until the ninth year, when its crop arrives." Leviticus 25:20-22

The Seven Sevens and Jubilee

On top of this layering of revelation in patterns of sevens, God placed another layer. God established a pattern of seven periods of seven years to be followed by a very special celebration. Why another period of seven? There must be a purpose! God is emphasizing something He wants His people to know and understand. The repetition points to the importance God places on His desire for them to know this.

As the people of Israel have been commanded to observe the weekly cycle of six days followed by a day of rest (seven days), and a yearly cycle of six years of labor followed by a year of rest (seven years), they were also commanded to observe seven periods of seven years (forty-nine years), followed by a year of special celebration called the Year of Jubilee.

> *"You shall count seven weeks of years, seven times seven years, so that the time of the seven weeks of years shall give you forty-nine years."*[48]

Beginning with the year of release from the captivity in Egypt, they were to begin observing this cycle of seven sevens of years. God has repeatedly used the number seven, and emphasized the observation of a period of seven cycles in days (the week), years (sabbath year), and years of years (the Jubilee cycle).

This Jubilee year was a very particular observance. It began with a special Feast Day called the Day of Atonement. During the Year of Jubilee, every person was to return to their original land and to their original family. Land that had been sold to another person was

---

[48] Leviticus 25:8

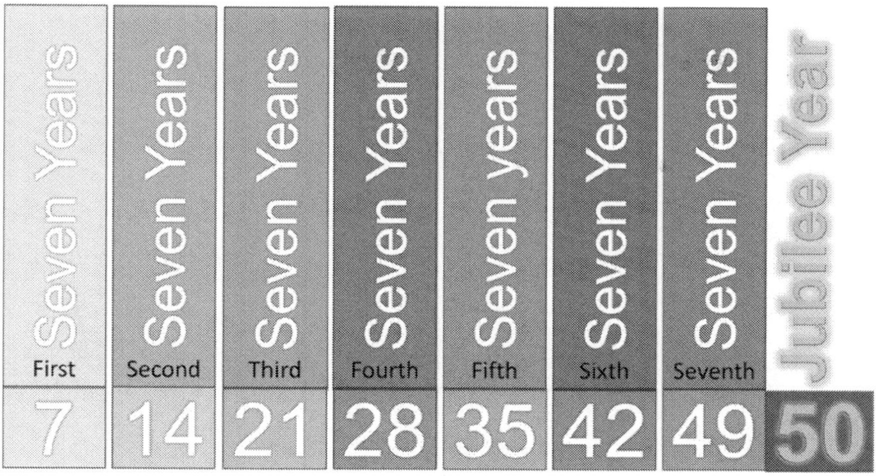

The Pattern Emphasized

Figure 9 The Sabbath cycle folded into sevens of sevens followed by the emphasis years of a Jubilee.

returned to the original owners. The land was purchased back. It was "redeemed."

When the people of Israel entered their promised land, the land God had promised to Abraham and by extension to them, God gave each tribe a specific piece of property within that land. When establishing this observance of the Jubilee year, God reminded the people this land was His.

> "The land shall not be sold in perpetuity, for the land is mine. For you are strangers and sojourners with me. And in all the country you possess, you shall allow a redemption of the land. "If your brother becomes poor and sells part of his property, then his nearest redeemer shall come and redeem what his brother has sold. If a man has no one to redeem it and then himself becomes prosperous and finds sufficient means to redeem it, let him calculate the years since he sold it and pay back the balance to the man to whom he sold it, and then return to his property. But

> *if he does not have sufficient means to recover it, then what he sold shall remain in the hand of the buyer until the year of jubilee. In the jubilee it shall be released, and he shall return to his property.*[49]

God intends for His people to know Him. He also ordains that we would know the things we need to know in order to know Him. He doesn't just leave us to flounder around in hopes of finding the knowledge He has dropped into the world. He purposefully places understanding, and then purposefully provides the means to understanding. He commands us to "know and understand", and also makes knowing and understanding possible.

For example: God is both the source of and provider of moral law and moral action. He desires that humans act in responsible ways toward one another and with the creation He placed them in. He then gives a moral lesson in the form of this law regarding property and ownership. We read the moral reasoning and morally right laws and out of that reading learn that God wants us to be moral. We have learned, and are now responsible with what we know.

However, the return of land to the original owners is anchored with a reason beyond moral reasoning alone. God claims the right to make this command over the land because of His ownership of the land. Certainly, as Author of Creation, He rightly claims ownership. As God, He is the ultimate owner of everything. But, we need to also see this as the rightful expression of legal, deed-holding ownership. God has given mankind ownership of land. I own the land I have because it has been purchased from a previous owner. God, however, still holds the rightful deed for all ownership of all of His creation.

The land of Israel, this particular, definable tract of property defined by boundaries and identified historically as the land of Israel, this land is claimed in a particular way by God to be His land. He hasn't made

---

[49] Leviticus 25:23-28

that claim over the tract of land my house sits on in Greenville County, South Carolina. He hasn't made that claim on the land defined as the State of South Carolina, or the Country in which it is contained. He doesn't have to. It is His. The only reason we have a country called the United States is because He has ordained it to be.

The land that Israel holds, though, has particular importance and purpose that no other country can claim. God made a particular claim to this specific piece of the earth as His. Therefore, no one could claim ownership beyond what He clearly identified as owners. God gave each of the twelve sons of Jacob (Israel) specific pieces of land when they returned to the land out of captivity in Egypt. He gave it to them. To give something legally requires ownership of the item. God gave each ownership. And then reminded them they were owners only because He had given it to them. It was an ownership as stewards over the land. He will return and claim all of it for Himself. This is an essential part of the answer to "Why six days followed by a day of rest?"

Why Six Days?

CHAPTER 9
THE PATTERN IN FULFILLMENT

Many Christians view the instructions regarding worship in the Old Testament as, at most, mildly interesting. Sure, if you're one of those theologian types, you might study the liturgical system God instructed the Jewish people to use. But, for the rest of "us", it's only the New Testament worship that really matters.[50] After all, we worship on Sunday because that is the day Jesus arose from the grave. Not much else really matters. Except, or course, the style of music.

However, if we remember that the God of creation is the God of salvation, that John tells us the same Jesus who died on the cross and arose from the grave on the first day of the week is the same person of the Godhead that is also the Creator of all things, it may allow us to look at the Old Testament a little differently. That same Jesus who fed the five-thousand using just two fish and five loaves of bread is the same person of the Godhead, in pre-incarnate form, Who wrote out the Ten Commandments into solid rock. That same Jesus who healed the man born blind is the same person who gave Moses the detailed instruction for the temple and for worship to be used there.

If I may use a little more sarcasm to help make the point, do you think it might just matter a little? Since God took the time to both give

---

[50] Yes. I am using sarcasm here to introduce an important point.

the information about how He wanted to be worshipped, and then has, by His sovereign power and providence, preserved that information for us to have today, perhaps it might be more than just historically interesting.

OK. So, God doesn't do things because He is arbitrary, or capricious, or simply likes to see how many rules we can follow before we give up. God does things with extreme purpose. He, in all of His ability, power, knowledge, is revealing Himself for His glory and our benefit. Since this is true, let's ask, and attempt to answer, a few questions regarding the Old Testament worship.

What did God establish as part of the yearly worship of the Jewish people? Why did He do this? Is there a meaning in what He is doing?

I hope you can already see that there is meaning and purpose. So, what is it?

The Appearance Feasts

Let's start with the "Appearance Feasts" described in the book of Leviticus. And, just to give you a hint, we should note there are seven of them. Yes. There it is again. Not because it is God's favorite number, or the "number of God". It is seven because God chose to use that number to bring Himself glory. For it to bring Him glory, the reason and purpose of the value of seven, the number of feasts, must be understandable. Do you get that? To bring God glory, we need to be able to understand why He chose seven. If we can't know why, if it isn't clear, then it doesn't bring Him glory nor bring us any benefit.

These feasts are established and described in Leviticus 24. And, they begin with the following command:

> *The LORD spoke to Moses, saying, "Speak to the people of Israel and say to them, These are the appointed feasts of the LORD that you shall proclaim*

as holy convocations; they are my appointed feasts. "Six days shall work be done, but on the seventh day is a Sabbath of solemn rest, a holy convocation. You shall do no work. It is a Sabbath to the LORD in all your dwelling places. [51]

Here is the six days of work followed by the seventh day of rest again used to emphasize two critical truths: First, that every day, every week, every repeated cycle of day and night, day followed by day, week followed by week, we are to be worshipping our God Who is the God of Creation. His identity as Creator is critical to the proper worship of God. Second, there is a "set apart" day for intense and specific worship on the seventh day of every week. God anchors what is to come next

	FEAST		*TIMING*
Spring Feasts	*Pesach* Passover	1st Month, 14th day (14 Nissan)	1 day
Spring Feasts	*Matsah* Unleavened Bread	1st Month, 15th - 21st (15-21 Nissan)	7 days
Spring Feasts	*Rashit Katzir* First Fruits	1st Month, 16th day (16 Nissan)	1 day
	Shavu'ot Weeks	3rd Month, 6th day	50 days later (the day following seven seven/s)
Fall Feasts	*Yom Teruah* Trumpets	7th Month, 1st day	1 Day
Fall Feasts	*Yom Kippur* Atonement	7th Month, 10th day	1 Day
Fall Feasts	*Sukkot* Booths	7th Month, 15th day	7 days

---

[51] Leviticus 23:1-3

with the designation of the week and weekly cycle of Sabbath worship. A cycle of six followed by a seventh.

God establishes and describes seven feasts that all Jewish men are to participate in. These occurred every year, throughout the year. They are, in order:

We are more familiar with some of these feasts because they correspond on the calendar with Christian holidays. Have you noticed that Easter seems to move every year? There is no fixed day, like Christmas which is always December 25th. Easter is linked to Passover in both the calendar and in what it represents. Unfortunately, for many Christian's, that is the limit of their knowledge of these feasts.

Since God gave these to the Jewish people, and we understand that in this giving, God is revealing Himself, there is benefit for us to understand each of these a little deeper. This will also help us understand what the relationship is, if any, in the number of feasts (seven, remember?).

Passover

The first feast is *Pesach* [*Pay-sahch*] (Passover). God chose to make this the first feast of their year. It inaugurated the Jewish holy year. This began their yearly cycle of worship. It was the start. The beginning.

The meaning is linked to the events of the Exodus, when the nation of Israel was held in slavery in Egypt, and God sent His deliverer to release them from their bondage. Following a series of signs, or judgements, on the Egyptians, there came the final judgement. This final plague, or judgement, was the death of the first-born. Only the households in which the doorposts were marked with the blood of the Passover Lamb were the first-born spared. They were delivered from judgement.

The meaning of *Pesach* is "to pass through, to exempt, to spare". This feast celebrates the deliverance from the culminating plague of judgement brought against the nation and leader of Egypt

In his Gospel, John records that Christ was crucified on the Passover[52]. And, not just on the same day. He was crucified at the time the Passover lambs were being slain in the temple. We may simply note that and pass on by, not realizing any significance that these two events occurred simultaneously. Or, because we know God isn't subject to circumstances, we understand and confess this was on purpose. God ordained that His lamb would be slain on the Feast of Passover, purchasing our deliverance from the judgement of death for our sin.[53] Now the purpose of the feast has much greater meaning than simply marking the historical event of deliverance from captivity for the Jewish nation. It was and is a revelation of God's redemptive work in history. It was prophetic. A foreshadowing of the coming Lamb of God who would be killed and His blood shed to deliver us from the death we deserved for our sin.

Unleavened Bread

The Feast of Unleavened Bread is linked to the Passover in timing, observance, and meaning. It begins the day after Passover and continues for seven days.

The Jewish people were instructed to bake bread for their escape from bondage. They would need food for the journey ahead. They had to prepare in haste, with no time for the bread to "rise". Their escape from the perils of slavery needed to be done quickly. They could not tarry and take their time. When the opportunity for escape came, it had to be taken immediately. With urgency. Just as our salvation. When confronted with our sin and the provision of the savior, we must not tarry, but flee into the promised land of His sacrificial gift of life.

---

[52] John 19:14 Now it was the day of Preparation of the Passover. It was about the sixth hour. He said to the Jews, "Behold your King!"

[53] You may also recall the events of Abraham and Isaac going up to the mountain when God was testing Abraham and instructed Abraham to sacrifice his only son to God. When Isaac asked his father, "Behold, the fire and the wood, but where is the lamb for a burnt offering?", Abraham replied, "God will provide for himself the lamb for a burnt offering, my son." (Genesis 22:1-14)

In homes that practice Judaism, this feast is celebrated through an elaborate practice of removing leaven from the home. Leaven is seen as symbolizing sin or uncleanness. All traces of leaven are carefully searched out, sometimes using a candle or flashlight, and burned outside the home.

Paul, writing to the church in Corinth encouraged those Christians to live holy lives, worthy of the Savior and God who has delivered them from the bondage of sin. Because God had redeemed them from their state of slavery, they were to live as ones no longer under the commands of sin, but under the Lordship of Jesus. He states,

> *"Cleanse out the old leaven that you may be a new lump, as you really are unleavened. For Christ, our Passover lamb, has been sacrificed."*[54]

Just as Christ was crucified on the Feast of Passover, fulfilling the prophet image of the sacrifice made to deliver us from God's judgement, his body lay in the grave on the Feast of unleavened bread. We are not only forgiven of the sins we have committed in the past. By the work of Christ, we are made able to stop sinning. He calls us to be without sin. To live lives of obedience.[55]

Beginning of the Harvest or First Fruits

On the third day after Passover, the feast of "First Fruits" is celebrated. *Rashit Katzir* – Beginning of the Harvest – is a time when the fruits of the first harvest are offered before God. The priest would take a sheaf of barley and wave it before the Lord. It was an offering of thanksgiving for the harvest yet to come based on the first fruit at the beginning of the harvest.

Paul, again writing to the Corinthian Christians, encouraging them regarding their faith, taught them that Christ is that first promise. His

---

[54] 1 Corinthians 5:7
[55] 1 Thessalonians 4:7 For God has not called us for impurity, but in holiness.

resurrection is the first fruit promise of the coming harvest which is our resurrection from the dead.[56] His resurrection is the proof and foundation of our faith and our hope.

Christ rose from the grave on the Feast of the Beginning of the Harvest (First Fruits).

Don't miss this incredible set of circumstances. God ordained these feasts with their timing and content and purpose, and then fulfilled each one as part of His redemptive plan that is running throughout the history of the world. The feasts were established at the time of the delivery from Egyptian bondage. Yet, God determined that the Son would inhabit human flesh, live, and die for our sins before the foundations of the world were laid.[57] As part of the revelation of God's plan, the redemptive work of Jesus corresponded with these Spring Feasts.

Pentecost (The Feast of Weeks)

Following the three spring feasts came the Feast of Weeks. Or, also known as the Feast of Counting, *Shavu'ot*. It is linked to the spring feasts in several ways. One of these is its timing. The "counting" reference is from the requirement to count from the Feast of First Fruits fifty days to the day of this feast. Or, the day after seven sabbaths ((7×7) + 1 = 50). This is also the source for the title "Pentecost", derived from the Greek word *pentēkostē (fiftieth day)*.

For the Jew, this is a celebration of the giving of the Torah, or Law. After escaping from bondage in Egypt, the Jewish people traveled in

---

[56] 1 Corinthians 15:20 But in fact Christ has been raised from the dead, the firstfruits of those who have fallen asleep.

[57] "And if you call on him as Father who judges impartially according to each one's deeds, conduct yourselves with fear throughout the time of your exile, knowing that you were ransomed from the futile ways inherited from your forefathers, not with perishable things such as silver or gold, but with the precious blood of Christ, like that of a lamb without blemish or spot. He was foreknown before the foundation of the world but was made manifest in the last times for the sake of you who through him are believers in God, who raised him from the dead and gave him glory, so that your faith and hope are in God." 1 Peter 1:17-21

the wilderness to Mount Sinai. They arrived there and prepared for and received the Law from God fifty days after their departure from Egypt. This giving of the Law was another freedom. While the Passover, Feast of Unleavened Bread, and Feast of First Fruits are all celebrations of deliverance from physical slavery, the giving of the Torah (Law) freed them from bondage to idolatry and immorality.

The "counting" echoes the pattern of the Jubilee observance. As there were seven Sabbath years (49 total) and then the Jubilee year, here there are seven Sabbath days (49 total) and then the Feast of Weeks. Celebrating the giving of the Law every Jubilee by returning land, freeing slaves marked the Jubilee celebration. Those observing these Feasts today mark the freedom from sin and idolatry the knowledge of God's Law brings.

For the Christian, we note it was on the Feast of Pentecost the Holy Spirit was given to the Church.[58] The Law does teach us how to live in obedience. But, it also teaches us our disobedience – that we are disobedient children. The external law (the Ten commandments and all of the law given in the Old Testament) teaches about God while it also shows us we fall short of God's design of Holy living. No one is able to keep the law. No one has except for Jesus Christ, the Messiah. And, until the law changes from external to internal, it would only act to teach.

God promised, though, that He would make the Law internal. The law would change from showing us our need for a Savior to evidence of the indwelling God. God promised that He would write the law on our hearts.[59] The Law of God would become internal. And, that internal

---

[58] "When the day of Pentecost arrived, they were all together in one place. And suddenly there came from heaven a sound like a mighty rushing wind, and it filled the entire house where they were sitting. And divided tongues as of fire appeared to them and rested on each one of them. And they were all filled with the Holy Spirit and began to speak in other tongues as the Spirit gave them utterance." Acts 2:1-4

[59] Jeremiah 31:33 For this is the covenant that I will make with the house of Israel after those days, declares the LORD: I will put my law within them, and I will write it on their hearts. And I will be their God, and they shall be my people.

The Pattern in Fulfillment

law would be used to truly free us from living in rebellion and idolatry. The indwelling Holy Spirit teaches us to live Holy lives. We aren't perfect. We still sin. But, the Christian with the indwelling Holy Spirit is now taught to live daily by being reminded, exhorted, admonished from this internal law.

> *But the anointing that you received from him abides in you, and you have no need that anyone should teach you. But as his anointing teaches you about everything, and is true, and is no lie—just as it has taught you, abide in him.*[60]

It is neither accidental nor coincidental that these New Testament events coincide with the Old Testament Feasts. It is not accidental or coincidental there are seven Appearance Feasts. It is not accidental or coincidental there are seven days of creation.

That last three Feasts are grouped together in the Fall of the year as the Spring feasts were grouped together. They are also different from the previous feasts in that God did not require any animal sacrifice as part of the Fall Feasts. Only the first four Feasts, Passover, Unleavened Bread, First Fruits, and Pentecost all had the requirement for a blood sacrifice.

God's lamb provided that sacrifice Himself during His first advent. He was and is the Lamb "slain from the foundation of the world".[61] Since God carefully and purposefully fulfilled each of these four Feasts in the life of Jesus Christ, shouldn't we expect the final three Feasts will be similarly matched in yet to occur events? Shouldn't our eschatology, or study of the final things (end times), incorporate an expectation of correlation with these remaining Feasts?

---

[60] 1 John 2:27
[61] Revelation 13:8 KJV And all that dwell upon the earth shall worship him, whose names are not written in the book of life of the Lamb slain from the foundation of the world.

Feast of Trumpets

Yom Teruah is the day of the sounding of the shofar or trumpet.

> And the LORD spoke to Moses, saying, "Speak to the people of Israel, saying, In the seventh month, on the first day of the month, you shall observe a day of solemn rest, a memorial proclaimed with blast of trumpets, a holy convocation. You shall not do any ordinary work, and you shall present a food offering to the LORD."[62]

It is also referred to as *Yom Ha-Zikkaron*, meaning day of remembrance, or *Rosh Hashanah*, the Feast of Trumpets. To some Jewish and Christian theologians, this day represents the celebration of the first day of creation. For the Jews, it is the beginning of the civil year, and it is the date from which years are numbered. It is used for counting to determine the Sabbatical and Jubilee years.

Because it is the first day of the civil year, this day is also a celebration of the first day of creation. As a celebration of the first day of creation, it would be the day used to establish all other cycles of Sabbath days, years, the Jubilee cycle, and feasts by counting from creation itself. Since God established these very specific days and times, it is important to observe them on the days He has ordained.

This represented the start of the Fall Feasts which were associated with the great ingathering of food with the fall harvest. Thus, a food offering was ordained by God. God was worshipped by confession that all produce of the fields was provided by God's providence. He gave the harvest. The workers went into the fields and harvested the fruit of God's provision.

---

[62] Leviticus 23:23-25

Yom Kippur

The Day of Atonement, or *Yom Kippur* is observed by Jews as the last chance to demonstrate repentance and make amends for sin.

> *"Now on the tenth day of this seventh month is the Day of Atonement. It shall be for you a time of holy convocation, and you shall afflict yourselves and present a food offering to the LORD. And you shall not do any work on that very day, for it is a Day of Atonement, to make atonement for you before the LORD your God. For whoever is not afflicted on that very day shall be cut off from his people. And whoever does any work on that very day, that person I will destroy from among his people. You shall not do any work. It is a statute forever throughout your generations in all your dwelling places.*[63]

This Feast is viewed by Jewish people as only for sins between the individual and God – not for making atonement from person to person. This is specifically ordained for making repentance and amends for sin between yourself and God. The "putting to end" of sinning and sins.

The command to "afflict" was not to induce physical pain. The meaning is to humble oneself. This was done by removing fancy clothing and replacing it with sackcloth. Instead of eating great meals, fasting was observed. Some might "sit in the ashes", confessing that nothing would survive the removal of sin from our lives. Sin touches everything. Sitting in the ashes represented that state of being as if after a fire ravages all your possessions. There is nothing left – only ashes.

This was the command in making an atonement. Not with the wealth and riches accumulated in life. No offering from the harvest or flocks. Not with a great feast and adornments. We have nothing, can

---

[63] Leviticus 23:27-31

bring nothing useful to make an atonement. Nothing to offer for payment of sins. We need a savior. We need the Savior.

Sukkoth

Here is an unusual celebration. Unusual in that it remembers back to the time Israel wandered in the wilderness and dwelt in booths or tabernacles (*sukkoth*). The word for the feast describes a dwelling place.

> "On the fifteenth day of the seventh month, when you have gathered in the produce of the land, you shall celebrate the feast of the LORD seven days. On the first day shall be a solemn rest, and on the eighth day shall be a solemn rest. And you shall take on the first day the fruit of splendid trees, branches of palm trees and boughs of leafy trees and willows of the brook, and you shall rejoice before the LORD your God seven days. You shall celebrate it as a feast to the LORD for seven days in the year. It is a statute forever throughout your generations; you shall celebrate it in the seventh month. You shall dwell in booths for seven days. All native Israelites shall dwell in booths, that your generations may know that I made the people of Israel dwell in booths when I brought them out of the land of Egypt: I am the LORD your God."[64]

It seems strange they should celebrate this. Or, that God would want them to celebrate and remember this. However, if we remember that something special was also present at that time.

This feast, in contrast to the previous feast, is characterized by joy, eating, and worship. It came only after the harvest. All the food for the coming winter and year had been brought in and stored. Provision for the coming year was secured.

---

[64] Leviticus 23:39-43

The booths were constructed of pleasing plants. Young shoots and fruits of ornamental trees would have included palms and citrus trees, pomegranates, and crepe myrtles.[65]

While the nation of Israel wandered in the desert and had only temporary homes to live in, they also had the visible presence of God. When they departed from Egypt, the visible presence was a pillar of smoke in the day, and a pillar of fire at night. God was with them. He dwelt with them.

This feast is a remembrance of the fellowship they had with God when He was tangibly, physically present with them on this earth. And it is a looking forward to the time when God would come and dwell again in a physical, tangible manner with His people.

In summary, here are the feasts laid out from first to seventh as ordained for the people of Israel to celebrate. And, their fulfillment in Christ.

---

[65] Keil and Delitzsch, *Commentary on the Old Testament*, comments on Leviticus 23:38-43.

Why Six Days?

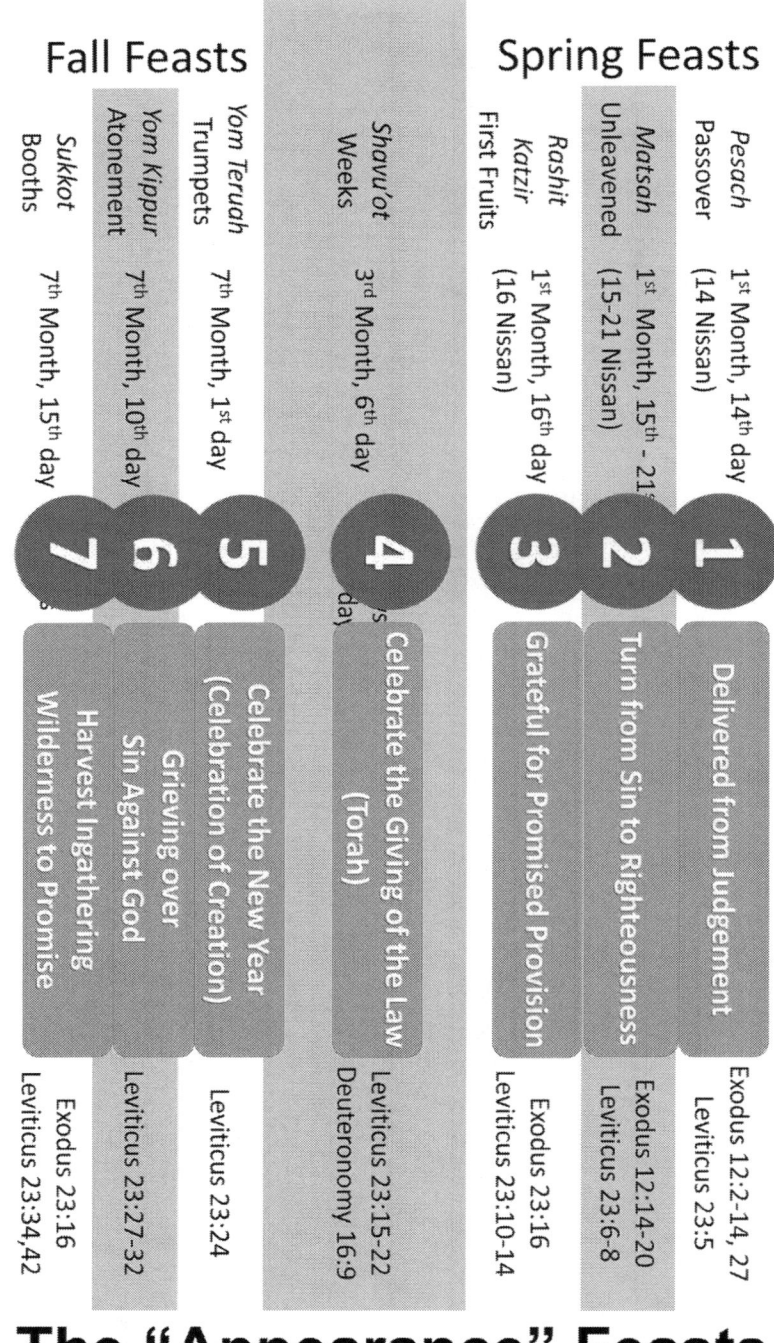

Fall Feasts | Spring Feasts

#	Feast	Date	Meaning	Reference
1	*Pesach* — Passover	1st Month, 14th day	Delivered from Judgement	Exodus 12:2-14, 27; Leviticus 23:5
2	*Matsah* — Unleavened	1st Month, 15th-21st (15-21 Nissan)	Turn from Sin to Righteousness	Exodus 12:14-20; Leviticus 23:6-8
3	*Rashit Katzir* — First Fruits	1st Month, 16th day (16 Nissan)	Grateful for Promised Provision	Exodus 23:16; Leviticus 23:10-14
4	*Shavu'ot* — Weeks	3rd Month, 6th day	Celebrate the Giving of the Law (Torah)	Leviticus 23:15-22; Deuteronomy 16:9
5	*Yom Teruah* — Trumpets	7th Month, 1st day	Celebrate the New Year (Celebration of Creation)	Leviticus 23:24
6	*Yom Kippur* — Atonement	7th Month, 10th day	Grieving over Sin Against God	Leviticus 23:27-32
7	*Sukkot* — Booths	7th Month, 15th day	Harvest Ingathering / Wilderness to Promise	Exodus 23:16; Leviticus 23:34, 42

The "Appearance" Feasts

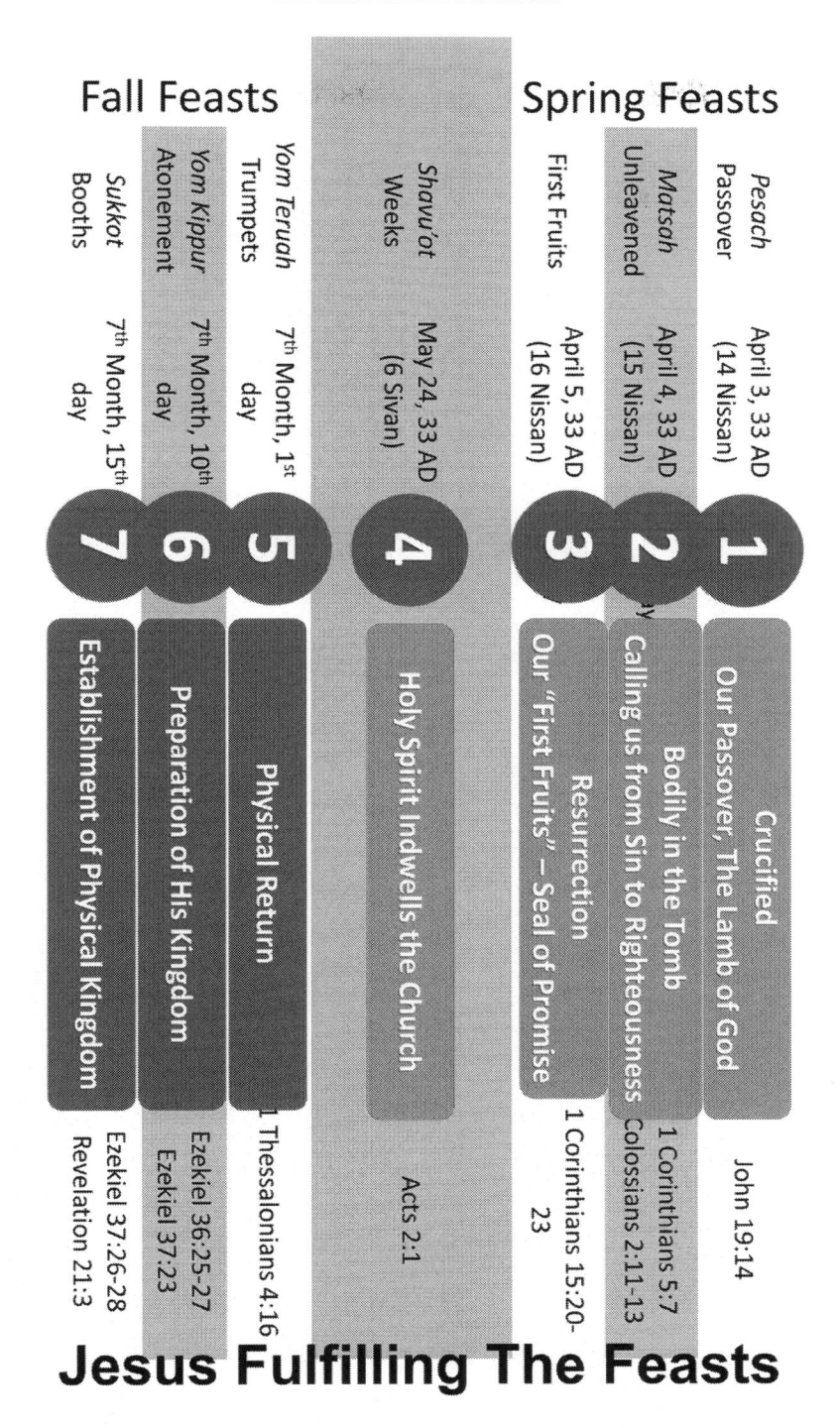

The Pattern in Fulfillment

Spring Feasts

1. *Pesach* Passover — April 3, 33 AD (14 Nissan) — Crucified, Our Passover, The Lamb of God — John 19:14

2. *Matsah* Unleavened — April 4, 33 AD (15 Nissan) — Bodily in the Tomb, Calling us from Sin to Righteousness — 1 Corinthians 5:7; Colossians 2:11-13

3. First Fruits — April 5, 33 AD (16 Nissan) — Resurrection, Our "First Fruits" – Seal of Promise — 1 Corinthians 15:20-23

4. *Shavu'ot* Weeks — May 24, 33 AD (6 Sivan) — Holy Spirit Indwells the Church — Acts 2:1

Fall Feasts

5. *Yom Teruah* Trumpets — 7th Month, 1st day — Physical Return — 1 Thessalonians 4:16

6. *Yom Kippur* Atonement — 7th Month, 10th day — Preparation of His Kingdom — Ezekiel 36:25-27; Ezekiel 37:23

7. *Sukkot* Booths — 7th Month, 15th day — Establishment of Physical Kingdom — Ezekiel 37:26-28; Revelation 21:3

Jesus Fulfilling The Feasts

Why Six Days?

CHAPTER 10
THE SABBATH HAS A PURPOSE, TOO

From the beginning of the creation, God created the Sabbath and purposed that it would be celebrated. To be precise, God established (created) a day of rest on the seventh day of creation. It is clear this is important to God in His revelation to us. It was a distinct day, different from the others. It was emphasized throughout history, more so than the other days of creation. He created it for a purpose, and then He used that created day, the Sabbath day, to emphasize that purpose. This emphasis is clear in the way God linked the day into worship. Particularly in the Ten Commandments in a way no other event is linked.

In the New Testament Gospels, we find events occurring on the Sabbath, including those which resulted in Jesus proclaiming,

> *And he [Jesus] said to them [the Pharisees], "The Sabbath was made for man, not man for the Sabbath. So the Son of Man is lord even of the Sabbath."*[66]

---

[66] *Mark 2:27-28 [added for clarity]*

Why Six Days?

The Sabbath became a stumbling block for the Pharisees. It also became a stumbling block for some Christians historically and in the present. God's emphasis of the Sabbath can be misunderstood and overemphasized to the point of making the observance of the Sabbath of greater importance than God intended. In doing so, it can replace God as the object of worship. The meaning God intended, and the purpose God designed, can become lost.

Observing the Sabbath today is primarily done in three broad ways. First, by those practicing the Jewish faith as prescribed in the Levitical laws. They observe the Sabbath as the seventh, or last day of the week, in a manner that emphasizes the worship of God on this particular day. Within Christian groups, there are those who worship God on the seventh day. Seventh-Day Adventists and Seventh-Day Baptists both are strict in their observance of the last day of the week as the Sabbath. The majority of Christians have followed after the practice of the first day of the week replacing the seventh as the day of worship. This practice is described in the 1689 London Baptist Confession:

> *[God] appointed one day in seven for a sabbath to be kept holy unto him, which from the beginning of the world to the resurrection of Christ was the last day of the week, and from the resurrection of Christ was changed into the first day of the week, which is called the Lord's Day: and is to be continued to the end of the world as the Christian Sabbath, the observation of the last day of the week being abolished.*[67]

---

[67] *The Baptist Confession of Faith of 1689 with Scripture Proofs, Put forth by the Elders and Brethren of many Congregations of Christians, (baptized upon profession of their faith) in London and the Country.* Chapter 22, paragraph 7.

Let me state again: I am not, nor am I advocating Seventh-Day Adventism[68], or Strict or Moderate Sabbatarianism[69]. Each of these obscures the value and worth of the Sabbath purpose by making the keeping of the Sabbath either a mark of personal piety, or a method to sanctification. If not heretical, any teaching that depicts my actions as producing sanctification should at least be understood as in extreme error.

The Sabbath is Part of the Creation

God is very clear about the Sabbath. He was clear about its purpose and function, and its observance. If there is confusion among Christians today, it isn't because God mumbled.

The Ten Commandments as recorded in Exodus 20 is the most common place we associate with the law concerning the Sabbath. If we begin there, we must also begin by noting how the Fourth Commandment is linked back to Genesis 1.

> *"Remember the Sabbath day, to keep it holy. Six days you shall labor, and do all your work, but the seventh day is a Sabbath to the LORD your God. On it you shall not do any work, you, or your son, or your daughter, your male servant, or your female servant, or your livestock, or the sojourner who is within your gates. For in six days the LORD made heaven and earth, the*

---

[68] Seventh-Day Adventism elevates keeping of the Sabbath as a sign of a person's personal salvation. They fall under the classification of Sabbatarian in this belief. However, because they are a distinct group from Reformed or Puritan Christians who hold a strict view of Sabbath observance, I reference them separately.

[69] Sabbatarians observe the day of worship, either the last day of the week or the first, in a manner that requires outward expressions. These include legalistic abstaining from activity that is normal for other weekdays – vocational work, pleasure (participating in or watching sporting events, watching movies, reading), or other leisure activity that is not associated with Christian worship. This is seen in the Westminster Confession of Faith of 1646 and confessions that came after that incorporate similar language regarding the observance of the Sabbath.

> *sea, and all that is in them, and rested on the seventh day. Therefore the LORD blessed the Sabbath day and made it holy.*[70]

There it is. As plain as if it were written in stone. And, just in case we want to argue this was only a temporary command, one that should and can be adjusted, allow me to offer two observations.

The first is not my original, but an argument many have raised. Since none of the other nine commandments are considered to have been done away with during the time of Christ, why is this one? Christ didn't set aside the command to not make any graven images, or be careless with God's name, or told us to stop loving our fathers and mothers, or any of the other commandments. Since they all still stand unchanged and unaltered, what about the fourth commandment makes it the one we can ignore or modify? When we are honest with ourselves, we have to answer, "nothing allows us to set aside the command to observe the Sabbath".

And, again, no. I am not proposing the reinstatement of corporate worship on the last day of the week. Many Christians recognize the first day of the week as representing the day of the resurrection of Jesus from being dead.[71] In associating our faith based in the proof of the atoning work of Jesus this resurrection provides, we celebrate the resurrection day with our corporate worship day. In addition, there is clear New Testament evidence the disciples met and worshipped on the first day of the week.[72]

---

[70] Exodus 20:8-11
[71] Matthew 28, Mark 16, Luke 24, John 20 all are very clear on the precise day of the week on which Jesus arose from the dead. It was the first day, or our Sunday.
[72] It is seen as occurring with the early church in their acts of worship:
"On the first day of the week, when we were gathered together to break bread, Paul talked with them, intending to depart on the next day, and he prolonged his speech until midnight." Acts 20:7
And in Paul's instructions to the church, and indication of the day on which they gathered: "On the first day of every week, each of you is to put something aside and store it up, as he may prosper, so that there will be no collecting when I come." 1 Corinthians 16:2

However, there is no good reason to set aside the seventh day of the week as no longer having any important place in the life of a Christian. Modern Christianity makes no more regard for Saturday that we do for Monday through Friday. Other than it is a day for us to rest from work.

For the people of Israel, however, the command to observe the Sabbath is critical in their relationship to God. This creates a theological-historical event for Christians, too. From that theological-historical meaning, we can understand the meaning and purpose of the Sabbath. That root of understanding will branch out into larger and greater understandings of God's purposes and actions. There is significant benefit to every area of our living and worship.

The observation of the Sabbath as a day of worship was specifically linked to a command that this observation should continue as long as the world lasted. Such as found in Exodus 31.

> *"You are to speak to the people of Israel and say, 'Above all you shall keep my Sabbaths, for this is a sign between me and you throughout your generations, that you may know that I, the LORD, sanctify you. You shall keep the Sabbath, because it is holy for you. Everyone who profanes it shall be put to death. Whoever does any work on it, that soul shall be cut off from among his people. Six days shall work be done, but the seventh day is a Sabbath of solemn rest, holy to the LORD. Whoever does any work on the Sabbath day shall be put to death. Therefore the people of Israel shall keep the Sabbath, observing the Sabbath throughout their generations, as a covenant forever. It is a sign forever between me and the people of Israel that in six days the LORD made*

heaven and earth, and on the seventh day he rested and was refreshed.'"[73]

God says this is a sign. A sign of what? That they (and we) are sanctified not by our actions nor earned by our obedience. The sign is to remind us, to teach us, so that we may know "that I, the Lord, sanctify…" The sanctification comes from God. It is His work. He doesn't tell us the cost. At least, not here. But, He is making a covenant to sanctify His people. The Sabbath is a sign of that covenant for all generations. It is a "forever" covenant. Well, that really messes up the "temporary" argument for the Sabbath worship, doesn't it?. But, wait. There's more. God says this sign that He made the heavens and the earth in six days and rested on the seventh is between Him and His people a sign that He will sanctify them.

It really couldn't be more clear. The creation in six days followed by a seventh day is a Gospel message. Keeping the Sabbath is how we confess that God created in six days and rested on the seventh. Keeping the Sabbath is a confession that God has promised to sanctify His people. It's not something we do to gain sanctification. It is a confession that God has promised to sanctify us.

In answering this question of "Why Six Days?", which we've seen is linked by God in a covenantal promise of sanctification in which we are commanded to keep the Sabbath, it is important to know "how" to help us understand "why".

God Rested on the Sabbath

What is "sabbath rest"? The answer of "Why six days followed by a day of rest?" necessitates we also know the meaning of the Sabbath. We must know what God means by "rest", and what being called to "rest" on the Sabbath means. This is going to be a challenge for us due to the confusion that has been associated with the Sabbath and what it means

---

[73] Exodus 31:13-17

to "rest". Just like the Pharisees, we must repent of wrong thinking and wrong actions to come to the truth God has clearly provided. To repent of wrong thinking, we must realize we've been thinking wrongly.

A Sovereign Creator

Young-earth creationists understand and teach that God stopped creating after the sixth day. There was and is no more creating that occurs. Progressive Creation and theistic evolution are the opposite. Each of these beliefs require ongoing creative events. The Bible clearly states that God stopped creating. What He created was good – He called it so – and by that proclamation He also declared it didn't need anything else. Finished. Complete. No more evolving required. No additional intervention to create modern humans. It was *good*.

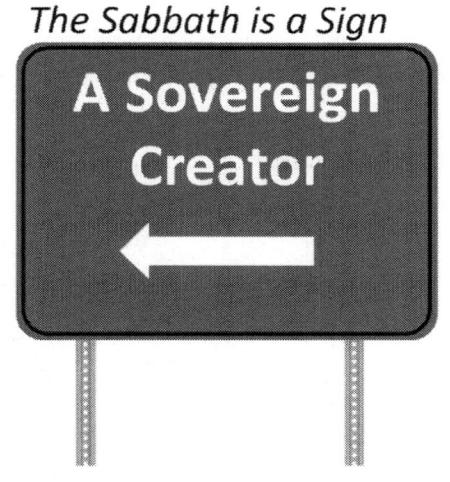

This is key to understanding the Gospel as revealed in the creation week. An essential component of Gospel comprehension is to know that working ceases. God's creative acts, as in creating new things that have never before been, all came to an end. All the animals, plants, creeping (some would prefer the word "creepy") things, stars, galaxies, planets, and humans were created in their ordained manner and state. God stopped creating. He ceased from His creative work. Not only did He stop because He was finished. God stopped because He is sovereign over creation. He stopped to establish a sign for us. Part of the revelation of Himself and of the Gospel.

As we acknowledge and comprehend that God ceased from working on the seventh day, we note that God linked this ceasing of work into the creation week. He makes it clear the celebration of the Sabbath is a sign between God and His people that He created all things in six days, and rested on the seventh. When we celebrate that pattern, it is more than a simple celebration of ceasing from work, or of taking a break, or of the creation week itself.

Part of the effect of the fall, of sin, is that now humans think we can be god. Or, we can achieve god-ness. Or, we can at least prove to God that we are worthy of His attention, blessing, and gifts. It is a common sin in modern society. Every time someone thinks or expresses, "God wouldn't reject me because I've done some good." Or, "There's a little goodness in all of us. God wouldn't reject us." And, the common heresy of "There is a little god in all of us. We are all god."

If you've not encountered those statements, you probably have encountered the question that often comes with tragedy. "If God exists and He is good, then why didn't He stop (insert any tragic event here)." All of these thoughts are based in the same idea. Humans have done good things that are worthy of God's attention. Our work, our good work and even our just plain work, should get God's attention. And, for those who are even better, they've done spiritual work. Fasting, religious observances, using the right essential oils and eating the right things. We are all working to achieve spiritual gold that we hope to trade for God's favor.

Yet, in the creation event, when God rested, He is showing that our salvation comes when we cease from our labors of self-righteousness. We must cease from working. Salvation doesn't come by our work. It comes by His.

The rest came at the end of the creation week. It seems so obvious that it is easy to overlook that God place the day of rest at the end. But, He did. It didn't end up there because God was controlled by the circumstances. You and I are controlled by circumstances. God isn't. God could have celebrated the creation by setting a day at the beginning or in the middle. This isn't just a convenience or because "well, you know, it should". Just because you may think that it's obvious the last day should be the day marking the week doesn't make it so. God placed the celebration of the sufficiency of the creative acts at the end not because it works best that way. He did so because that's where the message He is giving belongs.

While we are noting circumstances, how long does it take to "cease"? Is there any time needed? Do we say, "I was out fishing for six hours, and then it took me another hour to cease from fishing."? No. It is instantaneous. We just stop. So, why did God set aside a day? The day of "rest", of "ceasing from work", was the same length as each of the previous days. God did cease, but He didn't just cease. He established a day to commemorate, to celebrate, to reveal His rest. A full day, the same length as each of the previous days. He did so because the length is part of the message He is giving.

From the time of the exodus, through the time of the giving of the ten commandments, into the present, the Jewish people who practice the Sabbath observance, clearly link their observance of the six days of work and a Sabbath, to the six days of creation. They understood from before the time of Jesus, that they were confessing God's creation of the world in six days followed by a day of rest every time they celebrated the Sabbath. We can join them in understanding:

- The Sabbath Rest is confession of God's Sovereignty in creation.
- A confession of God's Sovereignty over the existing creation.
- A confession of God's Sovereignty over the timing and the keeping of time and the purpose of time in the creation.

Yet, more than all of these, the Sabbath points to salvation.

Rest Teaches About Salvation

God gave humans work as a blessing. Before Adam sinned, God placed Adam in the Garden of Eden, and instructed Adam to keep it. Adam was the gardener. His job, his work, was to tend to the needs of the earth. To subdue it and fill it. To use what God had placed as provision for mankind to use for God's glory and man's good. Before sin entered the world, work was given as a blessing. Good, fulfilling, purposeful, God-honoring work. Just as God had worked in creating, and that work brought glory to God, so does the right work of our hands bring glory to God. We are designed to produce good things. God worked. We work. God rested. We sinned and need salvation.

How are we to achieve restoration to fellowship with God? God declared that He would sanctify. And, He made that promise by pointing to His act of work followed by a day of rest, and commanded the observance of a day of rest just like He did. God is showing us that it is not our work that will bring salvation. We must cease from the labor of our hands. It is utterly insufficient. All of our work is now corrupted by sin. There is no work we can accomplish that will achieve the salvation we need. We must cease from work. We must "rest".

St Augustine, an early church leader and theologian whose writings are still impacting Christians today, made this very point in *The City of God*. The Sabbath is a picture of salvation.

> *"Most appropriately, therefore, the sacred narrative states that God rested, meaning thereby that those rest who are in Him, and whom He makes to rest. And this the prophetic narrative promises also to the men to whom it speaks, and for whom it was written, that they themselves, after those good works which God does in and by them, if they have managed by faith to get near to God in this life, shall enjoy in Him eternal rest. This was pre-figured to the ancient people of God by the rest enjoined in their sabbath law..."*[74]

---

[74] St. Augustine, *The City of God*, Book XI, Chapter 8, "What We are to Understand of God's Resting on the Seventh Day, After the Six Days' Work", http://www.ccel.org/ccel/schaff/npnf102.iv.XI.8.html, accessed January 5, 2018.

Israel Left Bondage in Egypt for the Promised Land

The account of God's deliverance of His people from slavery in Egypt is filled with theological truth along with the shadows and types of Christ. God's redemptive work is revealed in this work of freeing the Israelites from the bondage under the Egyptians. The deliverance is both out of something and in to something. They are delivered from slavery and into freedom. They are delivered out of Egypt and in to the land of Promise.

Along with the giving of the Law at Mt. Sinai, the testing of the people and their failure, the constant provision and patience of God is revealed. One of those revealed lessons occurred early in the journey. Before the giving of the Law. The people became hungry, and God provided bread from heaven. We looked at the significance of timing of the collection of manna already. In addition to needing food, the people needed water. They became thirsty, and God provided water out of a rock. As with the provision of manna, the water from a rock is filled with revelation of God's salvation.

> All the congregation of the people of Israel moved on from the wilderness of Sin by stages, according to the commandment of the LORD, and camped at Rephidim, but there was no water for the people to drink. Therefore the people quarreled with Moses and said, "Give us water to drink." And Moses said to them, "Why do you quarrel with me? Why do you test the LORD?" But the people thirsted there for water, and the people grumbled against Moses and said, "Why did you bring us up out of Egypt, to kill us and our children and our livestock with thirst?" So Moses cried to the LORD, "What shall I do with this people? They are almost ready to stone me." And the LORD said to Moses, "Pass on before the people, taking with you some of the elders of Israel, and take in your

> *hand the staff with which you struck the Nile, and go. Behold, I will stand before you there on the rock at Horeb, and you shall strike the rock, and water shall come out of it, and the people will drink." And Moses did so, in the sight of the elders of Israel. And he called the name of the place Massah and Meribah, because of the quarreling of the people of Israel, and because they tested the LORD by saying, "Is the LORD among us or not?"*[75]

Although the people had seen God's work in the miracles associated with judgement against Egypt and for their deliverance, they doubted. God had told them He would take them into a land of promise. It was their salvation. He would deliver them out of the hands of their enemies. He would save them. But, they did not believe, and accused God of not caring. When God promised salvation, they accused God of delivering death.

This event in Israel's history was used by King David when he wrote about the "rest" of God in Psalm 95.

> *7 For he is our God, and we are the people of his pasture, and the sheep of his hand. Today, if you hear his voice,*
> *8 do not harden your hearts, as at Meribah, as on the day at Massah in the wilderness,*
> *9 when your fathers put me to the test and put me to the proof, though they had seen my work.*[76]

David used this reference of sinful doubt and distrust of God as a reminder and a warning. He used it as a call to soften the hearer's hearts. He used this reminder of the sin of unbelief and the need to repent and

---

[75] Exodus 17:1-7
[76] Psalms 95:7-9

believe. Hard hearts are closed off to God leading to unbelief. Soft hearts are open to God leading to belief.

However, to really appreciate what is in this Psalm, you have to note this call to repentance and belief is anchored in a confession of God being identified as Creator. David calls for a confession of God as God. God is worthy of worship because He is the great God and King above all Gods. David relates this confession of greatest of great to God as the One Whom, "in his hand are the depths of the earth; the heights of the mountains are his also." And, using poetic tools, proclaims, "The sea is his, for he made it, and his hands formed the dry land." This call to repent from unbelief, and confess God for Who He Is uses God's identity as Creator to justify and motivate worship. The final stanza is a warning of the consequences of unbelief, "Therefore I swore in my wrath, 'They shall not enter my rest.'"

Rest is God's salvation. His provision. The place our labors cease. We no longer strive to please Him, or work to find favor, or struggle to gain righteousness. So, when the writer of Hebrews links back to this same Psalm, and says, "Therefore, while the promise of entering his rest still stands, let us fear lest any of you should seem to have failed to reach it."[77] It is clear "rest" is a reference to salvation.

Consider what comes next in this passage from Hebrews we previously encountered. This rest is linked to the creation week and God's resting on the seventh day.

> *For he has somewhere spoken of the seventh day in this way: "And God rested on the seventh day from all his works." And again in this passage he said, "They shall not enter my rest." Since therefore it remains for some to enter it, and those who formerly received the good news failed to enter because of disobedience,*

---

[77] Hebrews 4:1 It is profoundly important to recognize the link from the story of the people at Meribah, and the Psalm of David, and this passage in Hebrews. They all point to salvation.

> *again he appoints a certain day, "Today," saying through David so long afterward, in the words already quoted, "Today, if you hear his voice, do not harden your hearts." For if Joshua had given them rest, God would not have spoken of another day later on. So then, there remains a Sabbath rest for the people of God, for whoever has entered God's rest has also rested from his works as God did from his. Let us therefore strive to enter that rest, so that no one may fall by the same sort of disobedience.*[78]

Rest, then, is pointing us to a cessation of our labor. Our exertions come to an end. We must rest.

This is salvation foretold, illustrated, revealed. The Sabbath (rest) is established before man sins by an omnipotent God who knows that we will need salvation, but are utterly unable to achieve it. Therefore, God placed the gospel in the creation week. Before sin entered the world (after day seven), God had already established the day of rest which is a picture of salvation from sin. Also in the giving of the law. The Gospel which tells us we are saved by the work of God, not our work. We must "rest" from trying to achieve salvation. Within the very giving of the law, the Gospel is embedded in the fourth commandment.

Salvation comes not by the work of our hands. Cease working. Stop. Rest. And do this every six days. Preach to yourselves every six days that salvation will not come by your work, but by God's.

We have both a Sovereign Creator Who is our Sovereign Savior.

---

[78] Hebrews 4:4-11

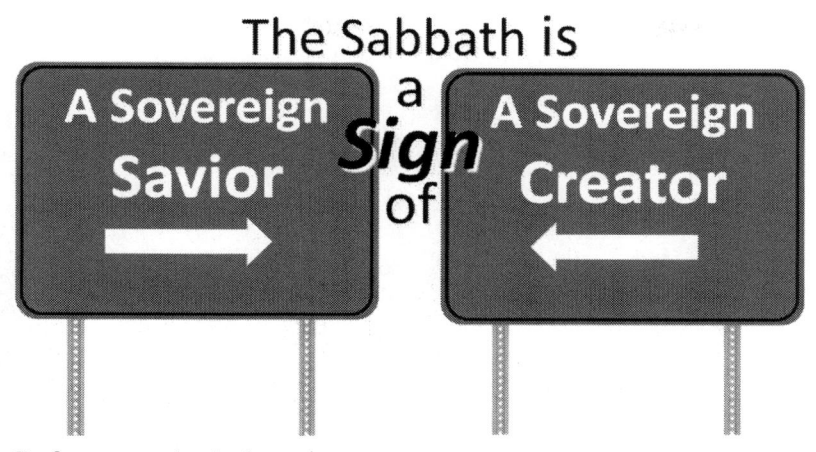

The Sabbath is a Sign of A Sovereign Savior / A Sovereign Creator

Before we miss it though...

Why does God place this reference to the seventh day of creation week, the day God "rested" and established the Sabbath here in this passage? And, why does God then say, "So, there remains a Sabbath rest for the people of God"? Avoid a hermeneutic shuffle. Use good, straightforward exegesis. What does the text say? It says that there remains a rest for the people of God. Who are these people? Certainly, the church. But, also the nation of Israel.

Before you throw down this book, and proclaim that any thinking theologian holds to an amillennial view and replacement theology, note the previous verse states, "For if Joshua had given them rest". Given who? The nation of Israel. This isn't a reference to the church. This is a clear reference, in context, and now greater context that goes back through Psalm 95, back to the rebellion in the wilderness, before the Israelites entered the promised land. It clearly is speaking about those events. "Replacementing" that into the church is a bit much to swallow.

What rest would Joshua had given? Entry into the promised land. To whom? To the nation of Israel. Yet, the writer of Hebrews is now saying this rest still remains. And, since it remains, we now have a clear answer to "Why Six Days?"

Why Six Days?

CHAPTER 11
AN ANSWER

Why Six Days...

As confident as a person can be in a conclusion based on careful study which guards against personal bias, I am confident in this answer. However, you'll note the title of this chapter. There are only certain knowledge I can hold with sufficient confidence for use of the article "The". The virgin birth of Christ. The substitutionary atonement. The truth of salvation by grace alone through faith alone in Christ alone. The days of creation are six, literal, 24-hour-equivalent days. These are truths that can be held without question.

This answer, though, I hold with humility, and confess there are great theologians as well as trustworthy Christian brothers and sisters who are going to disagree with this answer. There are men of God who will take exception to this answer simply because it disagrees with either their choice of eschatology, or another point of their theology. Mostly, disagreements will center on the status of the nation of Israel. Still, I believe it is the best answer of all possible answers. No other answer is consistent with a God who reveals Himself with purpose and precision. And, I am neither the first nor the only person to point to the following as the answer to the questions of "Why Six Days?"

The Days of Creation

The days of creation represent God's sovereign design over the history of the world. Six days represent six periods of time given for the dominion of man. For mankind to fulfill the design and purpose God ordained, as expressed in his mandate to Adam.

> *And God blessed them. And God said to them, "Be fruitful and multiply and fill the earth and subdue it, and have dominion over the fish of the sea and over the birds of the heavens and over every living thing that moves on the earth."[79]*

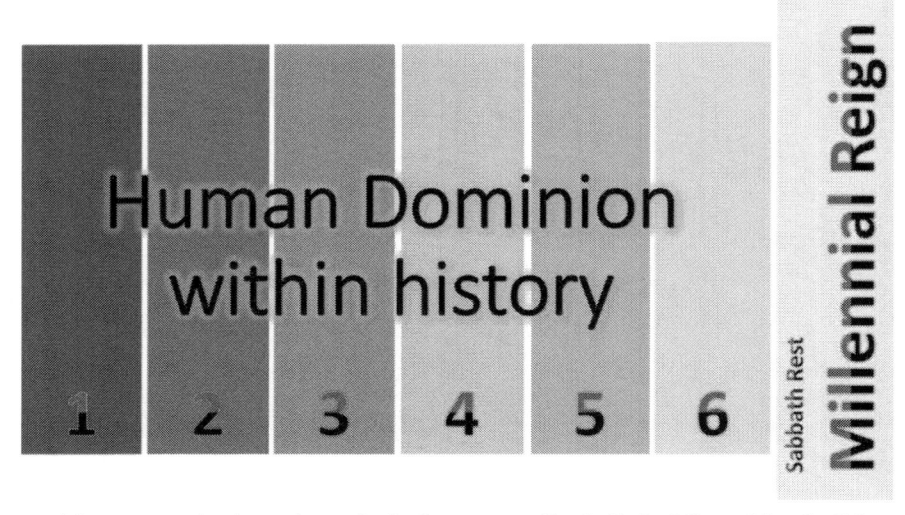

Human Dominion within history
1 2 3 4 5 6 | Sabbath Rest | Millennial Reign

The seventh day, though, belongs to God. It is His sabbath. Men will rest from their dominion over the earth. This seventh day

---

[79] Genesis 1:28

represents a seventh period of time known as the millennium. Or, the millennial reign of Jesus Christ.

The Millennium was Foretold[80]

Old Testament Prophecies of a Literal Kingdom

There are many places in the Old Testament where a future physical kingdom of Jesus Christ is foretold. Let's begin with this prophecy from Jeremiah.

> "Woe to the shepherds who destroy and scatter the sheep of my pasture!" declares the LORD. Therefore thus says the LORD, the God of Israel, concerning the shepherds who care for my people: "You have scattered my flock and have driven them away, and you have not attended to them. Behold, I will attend to you for your evil deeds, declares the LORD. Then I will gather the remnant of my flock out of all the countries where I have driven them, and I will bring them back to their fold, and they shall be fruitful and multiply. I will set shepherds over them who will care for them, and they shall fear no more, nor be dismayed, neither shall any be missing, declares the LORD. "Behold, the days are coming, declares the LORD, when I will raise up for David a righteous Branch, and he shall reign as king and deal wisely, and shall execute justice and righteousness in the land. In his days Judah will be saved, and Israel will dwell securely. And this is the name by which he will be called: 'The LORD is our righteousness.' "Therefore,

---

[80] It is not the purpose nor scope of this author to fully defend or exposit all eschatological positions. The discussion of the millennium, and the premillennial view are limited to application of the answer to the original question of "Why Six Days?". Curious readers are encouraged to study the eschatological views within theology with a mind to know God.

> *behold, the days are coming, declares the LORD, when they shall no longer say, 'As the LORD lives who brought up the people of Israel out of the land of Egypt,' but 'As the LORD lives who brought up and led the offspring of the house of Israel out of the north country and out of all the countries where he had driven them.' Then they shall dwell in their own land."*[81]

Here the prophet Jeremiah records the Words of God regarding the kingdom of the Messiah. The passage begins with a condemnation of the shepherds of God's people who have destroyed the nation. Their unrighteous leadership, their idolatry led to the judgement of God against His own people. However, there is clearly a statement that God will bring them back. He will restore the nation of Israel. This prophecy preceded the Babylonian captivity. Therefore, some may conclude this prophecy refers to the restoration from Babylon. Jeremiah prophesied the captivity in Babylon, including details of how long the judgement of captivity would last.[82] So, there would clearly be a restoration into the promised land.

However. This prophecy specifies a unique king of that restoration. Verse 5 uses a description that is a title of the king to come, "...I will raise up for David a righteous Branch,..." This is clearly a reference to the coming Messiah. The incarnate God who will reign, according to this prophecy "... as king and deal wisely,...". The first advent of Jesus, there was no coronation. Jesus was wise, and dealt wisely. But, not as a recognized and acknowledged king in a kingdom. The prophecy emphasizes the reality of this kingdom as real and physical. It is a kingdom in which this "righteous Branch" will "execute justice and righteousness *in the land*" (emphasis added). Although Jesus was both just and righteous, and all He did during His first advent was just and

---

[81] Jeremiah 23:1-8
[82] Jeremiah 25:8-12

An Answer

righteous, he did not execute that justice and righteousness in the land. The phrase clearly states this action as one who is wielding authority as the acknowledged sovereign over an acknowledged kingdom.

Although we may be tempted to view these statements as allegorical, and decide they apply to the ministry of Jesus during his first advent, there is more in the prophecy that should keep us from this. Verse 6 notes that "In his days Judah will be saved and Israel will dwell securely." During the first advent, Jerusalem was not secure, and Judah was not saved. It was under the rule of a foreign, pagan government. It was trodden down by an idolatrous nation, that ruled through force and power and strength over those they conquered. Israel was subdued and submissive. The title of the Messiah in Jeremiah was not applied to Jesus during his time on earth. He was known as many things, but never referred to as "The LORD is our righteousness".

It also cannot refer to the nation of Israel that exists today. Although that nation is a real, physical nation, there is no king, no Messiah, no "The LORD is our righteousness" keeping them safe. They are surrounded by nations who have sworn to destroy them. They receive attacks from missiles and terrorists on a daily basis. Therefore, here is a reference to "the days are coming" that are yet to come for us, also. A future time when a real, physical king who will be called "The LORD is our righteousness" will dwell in a real physical kingdom that he makes secure and safe. One in which He is the King.

There are a multitude of references to the millennial kingdom. A second example we will consider is in the book of the prophet Zechariah, chapter 14. Theologians agree this speaks of the coming "Day of the Lord", representing the second advent of Jesus, Christ. There are real physical events described as occurring in real space and real time in these prophecies. And, it is clear these have no place in history past that could be described by these events.

For example, consider the following event.

> *On that day his feet shall stand on the Mount of Olives that lies before Jerusalem on the east, and the Mount of Olives shall be split in two from east to west by a very wide valley, so that one half of the Mount shall move northward, and the other half southward*[83].

Either this is allegory with limited purpose of presenting essential theological knowledge, or it describes an as-yet not happened event. If it is an allegory, then the meaning should be clear. The purpose of the allegory, and the meaning of the allegory must be understandable, or the allegory fails and is useless. Any theological system that claims this is only allegorical is then faced with the challenge of described the clear, plain, and important theological knowledge God is imparting by the allegory. It's clear this isn't allegory. It is a real event.

It is followed by the prophecy that "the Lord will be king over all the earth."[84] It is true that Jesus is King now. He is sovereign, and sovereign over all the earth. But, why is it necessary to say He will be king when He already is king? The preincarnate Christ is no less sovereign during Zechariah's time, and no more sovereign following His incarnation, death, and resurrection. Therefore, if this statement is simply a spiritual statement, or description of His eternal sovereignty, then it is in error. Note that it says, "will be". When will Jesus be king over all the earth? Only if this refers to a real, physical, definable kingdom does it make sense.

Wait! There's more!

The prophecy continues to describe a consuming battle and consuming consequences to the nations that have arrayed themselves against the Messiah and His city (Jerusalem). They are defeated in battle and judged with a horrible judgement. But, then the most amazing statement is made.

---

[83] Zechariah 14:4
[84] Zechariah 14:9

An Answer

> *Then everyone who survives of all the nations that have come against Jerusalem shall go up year after year to worship the King, the LORD of hosts, and to keep the Feast of Booths.*[85]

This is an astounding prophecy. All nations that had previously made war against Jerusalem will now come and worship the King. And, this worship will include keeping of the Feast of Booths. God could have used any worship event, selected any of the Appearance Feasts. He could have instituted and referenced a new Sabbath worship. He could have said, "they will worship me using songs they have come to love the most." He chose to tell us of this coming event by anchoring it to the Feast of Booths. The feast of celebration of God "tabernacle-ing", or living with us.

If this was only allegorical or mystical in meaning, there is no need for all nations to keep this specific feast. And, the language is clearly literal. When the prophet proclaims this will be a recurring event, "year after year", we understand this will be a recurring event. Allegorically, we would only need to understand that all nations would celebrate the feast. Literally, we understand this occurs on a yearly cycle. Therefore, clearly, there remains the orbit of the earth around the sun. The universe continues as designed. But, now all nations – ALL nations – are worshipping God in a specific place. In Jerusalem on the specific feast of Booths, which signifies the real, tangible presence of God as He dwells with His people.

When is this going to occur? On the seventh "day" of creation. During the millennium.

For our purposes, there are two more compelling Old Testament prophecies. The first is in Zechariah. Here is a prophecy of yet-unfulfilled events. Of all the Old Testament prophecies that point to

---

[85] Zechariah 14:16

the first advent of Jesus Christ, this is one that clearly points to the second.

> *"And I will pour out on the house of David and the inhabitants of Jerusalem a spirit of grace and pleas for mercy, so that, when they look on me, on him whom they have pierced, they shall mourn for him, as one mourns for an only child, and weep bitterly over him, as one weeps over a firstborn. On that day the mourning in Jerusalem will be as great as the mourning for Hadad-rimmon in the plain of Megiddo. The land shall mourn, each family by itself: the family of the house of David by itself, and their wives by themselves; the family of the house of Nathan by itself, and their wives by themselves; the family of the house of Levi by itself, and their wives by themselves; the family of the Shimeites by itself, and their wives by themselves; and all the families that are left, each by itself, and their wives by themselves.*[86]

The Jewish people and the Jewish nation do not acknowledge Jesus as the Messiah. They have not yet looked on "him whom they have pierced" as an acknowledgement of who Jesus is. This phrase means more than a casual glance. It means they have fixed their eyes on him with intention and a "profound earnest regard"[87]. It is a look that confesses Jesus for Who He Is. This look is accompanied by an acknowledgement this Jesus is the one Whom they have pierced. Like the non-Jew who's sin was the cause of the need for a Savior. But, not like them in that they specifically rejected Jesus as Messiah.

None of these events have occurred. They remain for the future. Since they remain for the future, there must be a time when they will

---

[86] Zechariah 12:10-14
[87] Jamieson, Fausset, Brown, *A Commentary, Critical and Explanatory, on the Old and New Testaments*, 1871, commentary on Zechariah 12:10.

happen. When this detailed – yes, note the details – mourning will take place. They must be able to look upon Him. How will they do this? In heaven? Not if they are not regenerated. The reasonable reading is this event occurs on the physical earth when a real physical Jesus occupying real space and time stand before real people who then make this very real mourning.

Isaiah recorded a parallel prophecy of this same event.

> *He was despised and rejected by men, a man of sorrows and acquainted with grief; and as one from whom men hide their faces he was despised, and we esteemed him not. Surely he has borne our griefs and carried our sorrows; yet we esteemed him stricken, smitten by God, and afflicted. But he was pierced for our transgressions; he was crushed for our iniquities; upon him was the chastisement that brought us peace, and with his wounds we are healed. All we like sheep have gone astray; we have turned—every one—to his own way; and the LORD has laid on him the iniquity of us all. He was oppressed, and he was afflicted, yet he opened not his mouth; like a lamb that is led to the slaughter, and like a sheep that before its shearers is silent, so he opened not his mouth. By oppression and judgement he was taken away; and as for his generation, who considered that he was cut off out of the land of the living, stricken for the transgression of my people? And they made his grave with the wicked and with a rich man in his death, although he had done no violence, and there was no deceit in his mouth.*[88]

---
[88] Isaiah 53:3-9

Who is speaking in this passage? The first two verses of the passage (Isaiah 53:1,2) make it clear this is a Jewish speaker looking back on the Messiah, who was also a Jew, as the Messiah suffered as the lamb of God. Yet, this is something that occurs after, not during, the first advent. This is some future event when, in repentance, this speaker confesses the Messiah had come before, and was recognized for Who He was. The speaker is acting on behalf of his nation, his people, his tribe in a public confession. When has this occurred? It hasn't occurred, because it has yet to occur. When will it? When Jesus returns and establishes His earthly kingdom. This speaker, who is representing the Jewish nation, is looking on Jesus who "was pierced for our transgressions; he was crushed for our iniquities; upon him was the chastisement that brought us peace, and with his wounds we are healed." Not the past-tense language and present-tense identity.

It is reasonable to place these events in the coming "seventh day" of creation – the millennial reign of Jesus, Christ.

The Remarkable Confession of Job

Job is considered by many theologians to be the earliest post-flood book. The events are clearly real events about a real person who lived after the dispersion of nations at the tower of Babel (2240 BC), yet before Abraham (1996 BC). The suffering of Job, and the lessons he learned through his suffering have been used by generations of people to comprehend why the righteous suffer within the sovereignty of God.

Job lost everything. He lost his family, his wealth, and even his health. Some would say he lost his friends, too. When they came to "comfort" him, what they really succeeded in doing was to make his suffering greater by accusing him of sin. They needed to find a reason for Job's suffering that was rooted in his actions. His friends needed someone to "blame" for their own piece of mind. While Job was answering their questions and accusations, he is driven to make a remarkable confession filled with prophetic promise.

An Answer

Figure 10 The suffering of Job[89]

> *For I know that my Redeemer lives, and at the last he will stand upon the earth. And after my skin has been thus destroyed, yet in my flesh I shall see God, whom I shall see for myself, and my eyes shall behold, and not another. My heart faints within me![90]*

Has this event occurred? Job prophesizes he will stand on this earth. The one you and I are standing on today. He will stand here and with his flesh and blood eyeballs, look upon the flesh and blood Redeemer. Did this occur during Job's lifetime? No. Did Job look on the Redeemer

---

[89] From the Vignette by Loutherbourg for the Macklin Bible.
https://upload.wikimedia.org/wikipedia/commons/f/fa/Vignette_by_Loutherbourg_for_t he_Macklin_Bible_28_of_134._Bowyer_Bible_Old_Testament._Headpiece_to_Job.gif By Phillip Medhurst (Photos by Harry Kossuth) [Public domain], via Wikimedia Commons
[90] Job 19:25-27

before or during the events of 70 A.D.?[91] No. This event is still future to us. It has not yet occurred. There remains a real place on this real earth in which the real resurrected Job will look into the face of the real, physical Redeemer.

When will this occur? The reasonable answer is this statement of Job's is "yet to be fulfilled." It will be filled following the future resurrection of the dead, in which God reunites the redeemed with their physical bodies. This future resurrection is the one Paul encouraged the Thessalonians with in his first letter to them.[92] This resurrection occurs prior to the establishment of the earthly kingdom of God.

The Disciples Looked for a Real, Physical Kingdom

Not only is a yet-to-come, real, physical millennial kingdom clearly foretold in the Old Testament prophecies, it was clear the Disciples expected the Messiah to establish a real, physical kingdom when He was present during His first advent.

Matthew records Jesus teaching on the end of the age and His second coming. In Matthew 24, Jesus and the disciples were leaving the temple, and the disciples bring up the subject of the temple. More precisely, they "came to point out to him the buildings". A parallel passage from the Gospel of Mark notes the disciples were pointing out the wonder of the stones and the wonder of the temple. Do you suppose this was casual conversation? Were the disciples making "small

---

[91] In 70 A.D., the Temple in Jerusalem was destroyed by the Romans. Preterism points to this date as the date of the final fulfillment of prophetic events.
[92] "But we do not want you to be uninformed, brothers, about those who are asleep, that you may not grieve as others do who have no hope. For since we believe that Jesus died and rose again, even so, through Jesus, God will bring with him those who have fallen asleep. For this we declare to you by a word from the Lord, that we who are alive, who are left until the coming of the Lord, will not precede those who have fallen asleep. For the Lord himself will descend from heaven with a cry of command, with the voice of an archangel, and with the sound of the trumpet of God. And the dead in Christ will rise first. Then we who are alive, who are left, will be caught up together with them in the clouds to meet the Lord in the air, and so we will always be with the Lord. Therefore encourage one another with these words." 1 Thessalonians 4:13-18

An Answer

talk", or simply trying to entertain Jesus with talk? The temple was a magnificent structure. The historian Josephus recorded that some of these stones were forty cubits (68 feet)[93] long, and the pillars supporting the porches were twenty-five cubits high (42 feet), and made from a single stone.[94] Truly magnificent.

It is likely Jesus was leaving the temple for the last time before His crucifixion. He had been here on many occasions. For every year of His adult male life, he would have visited here for the feasts. Now He was leaving never to return. He knew of the coming destruction of Jerusalem and the temple by the Romans. When His disciples asked, His response to the Disciples isn't what they were expecting. They were shocked. He told them "there will not be left here one stone upon another that will not be thrown down."[95] The Disciples waited until they were alone with Jesus, away from the crowd, and then asked, "…when will these things be, and what will be the sign of your coming and of the end of the age?"[96] They are looking for the Messiah to return. And, they believe His return will be associated with the end of the age. In other words, that the return of Christ will end the present age and begin the next. The present age is this age in which humans have dominion. The Romans have dominion over Jerusalem. Yet, the Messiah will reign in the age after His return. After the Lord then teaches them all that is recorded in the following passages, it is clear they still expect Him to return and establish a real, physical kingdom.

Even after His crucifixion and resurrection, as much as this impacted what they had been thinking about what the Messiah should

---

[93] Conversions from cubits to feet used the Hebrew long cubit comparable to 20.4 inches. https://answersingenesis.org/noahs-ark/how-long-was-the-original-cubit/
[94] Josephus, *Wars of the Jews*, 5.5.2.
[95] Matthew 24:2
[96] Matthew 24:3. Matthew notes the Disciples asked Jesus privately. Mark, that they had gone to the Mount of Olives and only Peter, James, John and Andrew were present. Mark records the question as, "Tell us, when will these things be, and what will be the sign when all these things are about to be accomplished?" Mark 13:4

have been according to their theology, they were still unshaken in their understanding that Jesus would have a real, physical kingdom on earth. Just prior to ascension, the Disciples ask again, ""Lord, will you at this time restore the kingdom to Israel?"[97] They were still looking for the promised kingdom. A physical kingdom with a physical King.

Is A Thousand, A Thousand?

The length of the Sabbath day is not something Christians are confused about. Well, except for the old-earth view. The seventh day of creation was a literal day, with a recognizable cycle of dark and light. You and I would experience that day like every other day as encompassing a period of twenty-four hours. The length of that day was the same as the length of the preceding days. Each a recognizable length of one typical cycle of dark and light. The equivalent of a twenty-four hour day.

The length of the millennium is also knowable. The amillennial and post-millennial eschatologists insist it cannot be known because there is no such thing (the amillennial view), or we have been in it since the advent of Christ, and don't know when He will return.

The length of the millennium is seen in the final book of the New Testament, The Revelation of Jesus Christ. Before we read the passage, take a moment to remind ourselves that God is capable of saying what He wants to say. He doesn't stutter. He is clear beyond our ability to even comprehend the clarity. He is purposeful beyond our ability to comprehend His purposefulness. God says what He intends to say. God communicates what He intends to communicate. Oh, yeah. And, that same omnipotent God is able to preserve what He has delivered to us in way of His written Word so that it retains what He wants us to know without confusion.

---

[97] Acts 1:6

An Answer

The Revelation (book) records what we understand as a sweeping view of history. God's work in redemption is laid out, with an emphasis on the final days. After describing the judgement on the earth, John records an incredible celebration of rejoicing followed by the uniting of Christ with His bride, the church (Revelation 19). The Lord is then shown returning to earth, defeating and subduing all those who opposed Him. After the Lord returns, John records the following:

> *Revelation 20*
> *1 Then I saw an angel coming down from heaven, holding in his hand the key to the bottomless pit and a great chain.*
> *2 And he seized the dragon, that ancient serpent, who is the devil and Satan, and bound him for a thousand years,*
> *3 and threw him into the pit, and shut it and sealed it over him, so that he might not deceive the nations any longer, until the thousand years were ended. After that he must be released for a little while.*
> *4 Then I saw thrones, and seated on them were those to whom the authority to judge was committed. Also I saw the souls of those who had been beheaded for the testimony of Jesus and for the word of God, and those who had not worshiped the beast or its image and had not received its mark on their foreheads or their hands. They came to life and reigned with Christ for a thousand years.*
> *5 The rest of the dead did not come to life until the thousand years were ended. This is the first resurrection.*
> *6 Blessed and holy is the one who shares in the first resurrection! Over such the second death has no power, but they will be priests of God and of Christ, and they will reign with him for a thousand years.*

Why Six Days?

> *7 And when the thousand years are ended, Satan will be released from his prison.*[98]

How many times does something need to be stated before we understand that it means what it means? It is not reasonable to conclude that God meant something other than "a thousand years" when He repeats it six times in this short passage. If God meant, "a really long time", He is more than capable of saying "a really long time". Since He is capable of saying "a really long time" in a way that would be very clear to the recipient of this revelation, but chose to say "thousand years", a good hermeneutic would conclude God is meaning a period of a thousand years.

What Does This Mean?

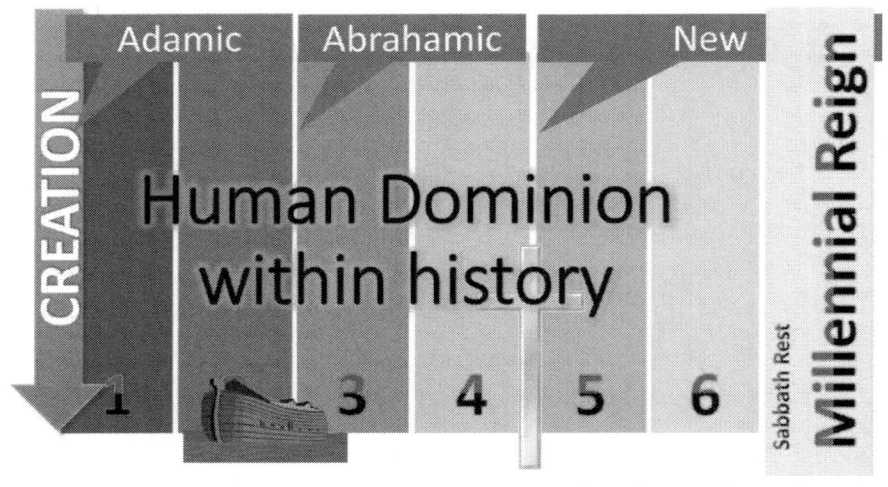

![Diagram showing CREATION, then Adamic, Abrahamic, New periods across days 1-6 labeled "Human Dominion within history", followed by Sabbath Rest / Millennial Reign]

The seven days of creation are set as a sign for all humanity of God's dominion over space and time. He has set six "days" for mankind to exercise the dominion God commanded. And, He has ordained a seventh "day" of 1,000 years in which Jesus Christ will reign over a real, literal kingdom on the earth.

---

[98] Revelation 20:1-7

An Answer

When overlaid with events from earth's history as described in God's Word, we may find correlation with major covenants associated with the "days". However, we need to move cautiously. Evangelical history is filled with the ship-wrecks of "finding what they were looking for". God designed us with the ability to see patterns. That's how we are able to see the face of someone and recognize who they are. It also allows us to see a complete stranger who shares familiar features with someone we know, and want to ask them if they are somehow related to that person. We assume they are related because they look similar. We see faces in inanimate objects such as electrical outlets and the sides of houses or a series of shadows on Mars. This phenomena, called pareidolia, is the product of God giving us the ability to see and understand patterns.

Unfortunately, we can find patterns and assign meaning when no meaning is intended. Numerologists and Bible Code (or Torah Code) enthusiasts succumb to the siren call of these patterns. In this trap we can find the Christians (and non-Christians) who have attempted to set a date for the return of Jesus Christ. William Miller, a Baptist lay preacher, used the prophecies of Daniel to extrapolate a date. Originally, Miller resisted setting an exact day for the Second Advent. However, he was pressed to be more precise, and published a date of October 22, 1844.[99] And, this is still occurring. Edgar C. Whisenant predicted a date between September 11 and 13 of 1988 based on a 40 year length for a "generation" and the use of trumpets for the beginning of the Fall Feasts.[100] Whisenant saw the establishment of the nation of Israel in 1947 as the start of a "prophetic clock". The adjustments of

---

[99] Wikipedia contributors, "Millerism," *Wikipedia, The Free Encyclopedia*, https://en.wikipedia.org/w/index.php?title=Millerism&oldid=835137705, accessed April 16, 2018.

[100] Edgar C. Whisenant, "88 reasons Why The Rapture Will Be in 1988: The Feast of Trumpets (Rosh Hash-Ana) September, 11-12-13", pamphlet published by World Bible Society, 1988.

the date in years following, instead of meaningful repentance, is a tragic warning against unrepentant error.

Therefore, let's proceed with caution. The goal is not to establish a day for the return of the Lord. The purpose of answering the question "Why Six Days followed By a Day of Rest?" is to show the days of creation as literal days contain God's revelation of His dominion over human history from a specific start to a specific finish. For that message to have meaning and be understandable, those days of creation must be literal, understandable days. The days of creation were each a single cycle of darkness and light that you and I, if we experienced them, would call describe as a 24-hour day.

When we look back through redemptive history, there are significant events. It would be wrong to assume God had no purpose for the timing of significant events He has recorded in His Word. These events are associated with specific covenants: The Adamic, Abrahamic, and New Covenants.

The Adamic covenant set in motion the dominion mandate. It was given at the beginning of creation, and at the beginning of the first "day" of history.

> *And God blessed them. And God said to them, "Be fruitful and multiply and fill the earth and subdue it, and have dominion over the fish of the sea and over the birds of the heavens and over every living thing that moves on the earth."*[101]

On the first day of creation, God created and separated light from darkness. It was the revelation of Himself. The giving of knowledge of God in contrast to the absence of knowledge of God. He revealed Himself to Adam and to Adam's race.

The next significant covenant is given to Abraham.

---

[101] Genesis 1:28

An Answer

> *Now the LORD said to Abram, "Go from your country and your kindred and your father's house to the land that I will show you. And I will make of you a great nation, and I will bless you and make your name great, so that you will be a blessing. I will bless those who bless you, and him who dishonors you I will curse, and in you all the families of the earth shall be blessed."*[102]

This covenant is marked by the promise that all nations would be blessed through Abraham, and is another piece or step in what has become known as the "scarlet thread" through the Bible of type, shadows, prophecies, and clear promises of the coming Messiah.[103] God confirmed this covenant, and gave details concerning ownership of the land in Genesis 15, confirming His plan that Abraham's descendants would occupy this land even though they would go into captivity in Egypt for 400 years.

Using the ages of the Patriarchs found in Genesis we are able to show Abraham was born in the year 1948 After Creation (A.C.), and died 2123 A.C. Isaac, the covenant son of Abraham, was born in 2048 A.C. The covenants given to Abraham occurred prior to birth of Isaac. Therefore, it is reasonable to conclude these were given around the year 2000 A.C. It would be reasonable, given the purposefulness of God, to speculate God made the Abrahamic covenant in 2000 A.C.

Let me encourage you to guard against writing off this argument as being tedious. Repetition with purpose has its own value. A slow progression through an argument designed to withstand cross-examination can be a joy to behold. And, avoidance of the traps associated with "finding what you are looking for" isn't trivial or God

---

[102] Genesis 12:1-3

[103] W.A. Criswell preached a sermon that became a classic book, *The Scarlet Thread Through the Bible*, that traces the redemptive work of God from the beginning of creation to the crucifixion of Jesus Christ.

isn't controlled by circumstances. He is the author of them. Therefore, the timing of the Messiah's first advent must be filled with extreme, or Godly, purpose. The Messiah's earthly ministry marked the presentation and giving of the New Covenant that was confirmed in His death, burial, and resurrection. Jesus' ministry, sacrifice, and triumph over death all occurred approximately 4000 after creation. This was the fulfillment of the covenant to Abraham 2000 years earlier. Jesus, as Abraham's offspring, is the ultimate blessing given to all nations. The timing of Christ's giving of the New Covenant occurs at the end of the 4th millennium after creation – corresponding to the ending of the 4th day of creation, and the start of the "last days".

These major covenants divide redemptive history – at least, so far – into three sets of two millennium each.

CHAPTER 12
WHO ELSE BELIEVES THIS IS THE ANSWER?

We are, by God's design, comforted when we discover that we belong. We want to be part of a group. Whether that group is a family, a church, a social organization. We need to know we are not alone. That's the purpose of this section. It isn't meant as an argument from authority or consensus. This answer and the premillennial view of Christ's return are orthodox.

In addition to Old Testament prophets and the Disciples of Christ, there were early Christians who wrote about the answer to "why did God create in six days followed by a day of rest?" Early church leaders who understood that the days of creation outlined human history with the culmination of an earthly physical kingdom of Jesus Christ. It was also a common belief in the pre-modern area. And, there are contemporary, respected pastors and theologians who hold to a premillennial view of eschatology.

These are just a few.

Early Church Fathers

It is helpful to remember the early church considered "the Bible" to be the Old Testament cannon. They were greatly influenced by the letters of Paul and of John, including *The Revelation*. These writings were understood to be inspired by the Holy Spirit, and containing essential revelation. But, they didn't have the collection of 66 books as we do today. The early church had the Psalms, the Pentateuch (Genesis, Exodus, Leviticus, and Deuteronomy), the Prophets, and the Books of Wisdom, along with the Gospels and New Testament letters.

With all these writings, many theologians note the early church placed greater emphasis on the Old Testament books for their theology, along with oral statements carried from place to place by their elders.[104] Their understanding of the end times (eschatology) had a common belief in the end of the earth preceded by a real, physical kingdom of Jesus that was centered in Jerusalem. This kingdom would last for 1,000 years. This common view was referred to as the chiliastic view, using the Greek work χίλιοι (khílioi) for "thousand". Both millennialism and chiliasm originally referred to the common belief in a literal 1,000 year reign. Millennial is the later Latin word for the earlier Greek word. Both describe the value of 1,000.

This teaching of the end of the earth after 6,000 years which was foreshadowed or foretold from the six days of creation was a belief common to the early church.[105,106] Let's consider a few of the early church leaders who taught or wrote about this.

---

[104] Fredricksen, Paula, "Apocalypse and Redemption in Early Christianity: From John of Patmos to Augustine of Hippo", *Vigiliae Christianae* 45 (1991), Brill, p. 169, (referencing Eusebius, *Historia Ecclesiastica* 3.39,12).
[105] Daley, Brian E., *The Hope of the Early Church: A Handbook of Patristic Eschatology*, Cambridge, Cambridge University Press, 1991, p. 39.
[106] Fredricksen, Paula, p. 152.

Who Else Believes This Is the Answer?

The Epistle of Barnabas (100 – 130 A.D.)

This early letter to the Christian church contains a clear statement of the relationship between the days of creation and the history of the earth. Although the title implies a known authorship, the identity of the writer of this letter isn't clear. It has been attributed to the Apostle Barnabas (a minor view), Barnabas of Alexandria, or some other unknown writer.[107] Although this letter is not part of the New Testament canon, and the author is unknown, it is regarded as an authentic letter based on current analysis, and was considered authentic and valuable teaching by other early church fathers.

Even though the identity of the author isn't clear, the message of the author is. It is a message of encouragement, teaching the recipients what it means to live Godly lives in a fallen world. The author uses the Old Testament laws and practices to illustrate how we should live. The writer linked proper living to proper understanding of God's work. In that work, God had told of the coming Messiah, who would then come again a second time. The Ten Commandments, circumcisions, and the Sabbath, all point to God's providential plan of salvation, redemption, and living as obedient servants of God.

The question of Sabbath worship was a critical one to early Christians. Therefore, the writer reaches back into the Old Testament teachings to help these Christians in understanding the meaning and practice of Sabbath worship.

> *"He speaks of the Sabbath at the beginning of the Creation, 'And God made in six days the works of his hands and on the seventh day he made an end, and rested in it and sanctified it'. Notice, children, what is the meaning of 'He made an end in six days'? He means this: that the Lord will make an end of*

---

[107] Schaff, Philip, *Ante-Nicene Fathers, Volume 1: The Apostolic Fathers with Justin Martyr and Irenaeus*, "Introductory Note to the Epistle of Barnabas", 1885. Accessed from The Christian Classics Ethereal Library, http://www.ccel.org/ccel/schaff/anf01.vi.i.html.

> *everything in six thousand years, for a day with him means a thousand years. And he himself is my witness when he says, 'Lo, the day of the Lord shall be as a thousand years.' So then, children, in six days, that is in six thousand years, everything will be completed. 'And he rested on the seventh day.' This means, when his Son comes he will destroy the time of the wicked one, and will judge the godless, and will change the sun and the moon and the stars, and then he will truly rest on the seventh day."*[108]

If this teaching was heretical, or even erroneous, we should find it refuted and contradicted by other church elders and pastors. We see correction of wrong teaching in the letters of Paul, and Peter, and James, and other church fathers. Sometimes the rebukes are very strong, while others are gentle.[109] Strong rebuke is for heretical teaching, the more gentle for error that needs correction, but is less of a threat. We do not find any correction of this teaching as stated in the Epistle of Barnabas. Even though this letter was widely available, and referenced by other church leaders, there is no indication of error.

It is important to acknowledge this association of six days with six thousand years didn't just show up or appear in 100 A.D. It is reasonable to conclude that other Christians were talking and teaching this same doctrine or idea. Yet, we do not find the teaching addressed as wrong or error. Not until the concept of a "no-millennium", or

---

[108] Epistle of Barnabas, William Wake translation, from The Suppressed Gospels and Epistles of the Original New Testament of Jesus the Christ, William Hone, 1821.
https://en.wikisource.org/wiki/The_suppressed_Gospels_and_Epistles_of_the_original_New_Testament_of_Jesus_the_Christ

[109] Paul writing to the church in Philippi is an excellent example. He didn't name the disagreement, or identify one group as correct and another as wrong. Instead, he gently exhorted peace for the sake of the Gospel.
"I entreat Euodia and I entreat Syntyche to agree in the Lord. Yes, I ask you also, true companion, help these women, who have labored side by side with me in the gospel together with Clement and the rest of my fellow workers, whose names are in the book of life." Philippians 4:2-3

Who Else Believes This Is the Answer?

amillennial view arose was the teaching of a thousand year reign of Jesus on the earth disputed.

Hippolytus of Rome (170 – 235 A.D.)

Hippolytus of Rome is another important early church father who clearly taught the days of creation represented God's ordination of six thousand years of human dominion followed by a millennial reign of Jesus Christ. He is known from and for the many books he wrote. *The Refutation of all Heresies*, is considered to be his principal work. However, his *Commentary on the Prophet Daniel* is the most complete and considered to be the best preserved.[110] In it, Hippolytus unambiguously explains why God created in six days and rested on the seventh.

> "But that we may not leave our subject at this point undemonstrated, we are obliged to discuss the matter of the times, of which a man should not speak hastily, because they are a light to him. For as the times are noted from the foundation of the world, and reckoned from Adam, they set clearly before us the matter with which our inquiry deals. For the first appearance of our Lord in the flesh took place in Bethlehem, under Augustus, in the year 5500; and He suffered in the thirty-third year. And 6,000 years must needs be accomplished, in order that the Sabbath may come, the rest, the holy day "on which God rested from all His works." For the Sabbath is the type and emblem of the future kingdom of the saints, when they "shall reign with Christ," when He comes from heaven, as John says in his Apocalypse: for "a day with the Lord is as a thousand years." Since, then, in six days God made all things, it follows that 6,000 years must be

---

[110] Cross, F. L. (2005). *The Oxford Dictionary of the Christian Church*. Oxford University Press

> *fulfilled. And they are not yet fulfilled, as John says: "five are fallen; one is," that is, the sixth; "the other is not yet come."*[111]

Hippolytus was also one of the early church fathers to teach the return of Jesus was not imminent.[112] He believed Jesus would return in 500 A.D. based on the date of creation set at 5,500 B.C (derived from the Septuagint), giving a total of 6,000 years.

Lucius Caecilius Firmianus Lactantius (250 – 325)

Lactantius is an early theologian who also held the millennial view of eschatology. He was born into a pagan family, and rose to become a professor of rhetoric in Nicomedia under appointment from the Roman Emperor Diocletian.[113] This same Diocletian who would later became famous for his persecution of Christians.

Similar to other early church fathers' writings, Lactantius wrote to encourage Christians to fully live the Gospel outwardly in their culture. We, as modern Christians, are attuned to encouragement and instruction built out of an emphasis on feelings or emotionally anchored argument. Lactantius introduces his treatise on theology, *The Divine Institutes*, by acknowledging the value of knowing above any other treasure. Not knowledge from any source. But, knowledge that represented true knowledge, good knowledge, helpful knowledge.

Lactantius also refuted asceticism[114] as the best way to knowing and understanding. There were, and are, examples of individuals who gave

---

[111] Hippolytus of Rome, *The interpretation by Hippolytus, (bishop) of Rome, of the visions of Daniel and Nebuchadnezzar, taken in conjunction*. (c. 202-204 A.D.) http://www.earlychristianwritings.com/text/hippolytus-exegetical.html

[112] David G. Dunbar, "The Delay of the Parousia in Hippolytus", *Vigiliae Christianae* 37 (1983), E. J. Brill, Leiden, p. 313, http://www.jstor.org/stable/1583543.

[113] Schaff, Philip, *Ante Nicene Fathers*, Book 7: "Fathers of the Third and Fourth Centuries: Lactantius, Venantius, Aserius, Victorinus, Dionysius, Apostolic Teaching and Constitutions, Homily", Christian Classics Ethereal Library, http://www.ccel.org/ccel/schaff/anf07.iii.i.html, accessed January 14, 018.

[114] Asceticism is the philosophy that ultimate understanding can only be obtained by denying oneself pleasure. In particular, pleasure associated with the senses.

up earthly pleasure in the assumption that giving up lesser things would gain them access to greater things. Give them access to the best knowledge. But, just as Augustine would do, Lactantius refutes this false pursuit, and denies the belief we can obtain truth and understanding by our own abilities and perceptions. Only by the work of God can we obtain what is valuable. Only by God revealing truth to humans will we be able to know truth.

Lactantius also refuted other worldly philosophies and ideas, including those of Plato, who taught the earth was exceedingly old. Plato did this, as he did with all he thought was ultimately true and correct, by relying solely on his individual intellect. Lactantius showed that in contrast, God has revealed the earth was created by God in a time scale that God had also made clear in His creation. And, God revealed from the beginning of creation that He had ordained a limit to the days of the earth.

> *"Therefore, since all the works of God were completed in six days, the world must continue in its present state through six ages, that is, six thousand years. For the great day of God is limited by a circle of a thousand years, as the prophet shows, who says "In Thy sight, O Lord, a thousand years are as one day." And as God labored during those six days in creating such great works, so His religion and truth must labor during these six thousand years, while wickedness prevails and bears rule. And again, since God, having finished His works, rested the seventh day and blessed it, at the end of the six thousandth year all wickedness must be abolished from the earth, and righteousness reign for a thousand years; and there must be tranquility and rest from the labors which the*

Why Six Days?

world now has long endured. But how that will come to pass I will explain in its order."[115]

Just as with the other written works we have from these early Christians, this statement is written in such a manner as to suggest Lactantius is writing normal, accepted, non-controversial teaching of these truths. He is doing nothing more than exegeting from scripture. This is not new revelation, or personal revelation. He treats it as something that has been known since the creation of the world, and is readily available and acceptable knowledge in his day.

Augustine of Hippo (354 – 430 A.D.)

Augustine's *The City of God Against the Pagans* stands as a monumental work alongside of his *Confessions*. In *The City of God*, Augustine wrote to defend Christianity against the false arguments raised by pagan religions to discredit Christians. He does so by first contradicting the pagan accusation that Christians were causing great calamities in the world, and then by setting down a defense of Christian belief.

Figure 11 Drawing of Augustine writing "The City of God" from a copy of the book published in 1475. Note the two cities depicted underneath. Public Domain.

---

[115] Schaff, Philip, *Ante Nicene Fathers*, Book 7: "Fathers of the Third and Fourth Centuries: Lactantius, Venantius, Aserius, Victorinus, Dionysius, Apostolic Teaching and Constitutions, Homily", Christian Classics Ethereal Library, Chap. XIV.—*Of the First and Last Times of the World*. http://www.ccel.org/ccel/schaff/anf07.iii.ii.vii.xiv.html , accessed January 14, 018.

Who Else Believes This Is the Answer?

This defense is contained within a wonderful structure of Augustine's describing the City of God, representing God's work throughout human history, and contrasting it with the city of the world as representing mankind's rebellious and self-promoting history. The conflict between these two "cities" is the theme of Augustine's defense of Christian belief.

Augustine moves from the origins of the two cities, through their history, and to the destinies of each as outlined in the God's revealed Word. Beginning with the origin of each city, he refutes the fallacy of pagan belief in ancient ages for the world based his understanding from scripture that the world will only last 6,000 years.[116] This 6,000 year length is derived from the six days of creation foretelling 6,000 years of history. In defending that claim, Augustine contrasts worldly historians, which he notes are untrustworthy, with the ultimate historian, the God of Creation.

These two cities are in conflict regarding the ultimate end of mankind. While different worldly philosophies point to an unknown future, the City of God culminates in judgement and God bringing an end to the present creation, and opening a new creation. The last judgement is accompanied by two resurrections. The first resurrection of Christians comes at the beginning of a physical kingdom of Jesus Christ. The second at the end of this reign on earth. These two resurrections are preceded by the six thousand years of earth's history. Augustine clearly describes the six days of creation representing six thousand years to be followed by the seventh day which represents the millennial reign. He incorporates this view of creation and history as if it is the clear and common understanding in Christian thought. Using a passage from Revelation 20, Augustine describes this relationship of the days of creation to earth history.

---

[116] In Chapter 40 of The City of God, Augustine contrasts the Egyptian claim their civilization has lasted for more than a hundred thousand years with the Biblical limit of 6,000 years for all of humankind. "For as it is not yet six thousand years since the first man, who is called Adam,..." p.880

> *"Those who, on the strength of this passage, have suspected that the first resurrection is future and bodily, have been moved, among other things, specially by the number of a thousand years, as if it were a fit thing that the saints should thus enjoy a kind of Sabbath-rest during that period, a holy leisure after the labors of the six thousand years since man was created, and was on account of his great sin dismissed from the blessedness of paradise into the woes of this mortal life, so that thus, as it is written, "One day is with the Lord as a thousand years, and a thousand years as one day," there should follow on the completion of six thousand years, as of six days, a kind of seventh-day Sabbath in the succeeding thousand years; and that it is for this purpose the saints rise, viz., to celebrate this Sabbath. And this opinion would not be objectionable, if it were believed that the joys of the saints in that Sabbath shall be spiritual, and consequent on the presence of God; for I myself, too, once held this opinion."*[117]

Pre-Modern Theologians

Alfonso X of Castile and Leon (1221 – 1284)

Alfonso X is also known as Alfonso the Wise and Alfonso the Learned. He was king of the Castile and Leon (historic regions of

---

[117] St. Augustine, *The City of God*, Book XX, "Argument – Concerning the Last Judgement, and the Declarations Regarding it in the Old and New Testaments", Chapter 7, "What is Written in the Revelation of John Regarding the Two Resurrections, and the Thousand Years, and What May Reasonably Be Held on These Points", http://www.ccel.org/ccel/schaff/npnf102.iv.XX.7.html#fna_iv.XX.7-p4.2, accessed January 5, 2018.

northwestern Spain) from 1252 – 1284.[118] The titular reference to "the Wise" or "the Learned" derives from his emphasis on a culture of knowledge in his court. Along with Christian scholars, he welcomed Jewish and Muslim scholars to work together in pursuit of greater learning and knowledge.[119,120]

Alfonso may be best known for astronomical tables attributed to him. These tables were compiled under his sponsorship, and became the source of later astronomic and scientific discoveries. In addition to these tables, Alfonso is known for the *Gran e general estoria*, or General Estoria (universal world history). Like Augustine, Alfonso divided the history of the world into six ages. It is not unreasonable to conclude this reflects the creation of the world in six days.

Christopher Columbus

Yes. That Christopher Columbus. The same explorer who traveled to the Americas in 1492. That Christopher Columbus who is the target of cultural correction that has wrongly labeled him a criminal against humanity. The truth is Columbus was a deeply religious man who studied the Bible extensively and wrote many books during his life. Of those, his book of prophecies has only recently been translated into English. Stephen W. Brown, in the prologue to this modern translation, observed that Columbus' Christianity has been ignored in modern history.

> *"For 500 years, the secular mind-set of the Western World has created a large body of literature about*

---

[118] The Editors of Encyclopedia Britannica, "Alfonso X", Encyclopaedia Britannica online, https://www.britannica.com/biography/Alfonso-X, accessed January 5, 2018.
[119] Wikipedia contributors, "Alfonso X of Castile," *Wikipedia, The Free Encyclopedia*, https://en.wikipedia.org/w/index.php?title=Alfonso_X_of_Castile&oldid=818427525 (accessed January 5, 2018).
[120] Frank Callcott, Ph.D., *The Supernatural in Early Spanish Literature Studied in the Works of the Court of Alfonso X, el Sabio*, Instituto de las Espanas, New York, 1923, p. 24

Why Six Days?

Columbus-sometimes with praise and sometimes with condemnation-but very rarely with reference to the essence of what motivated him, to wit, his deep and enduring faith in Jesus Christ."[121]

Without doubt, this deep and enduring faith both motivated and guided Columbus as he studied scripture and the writings of other theologians. Following his third and final voyage to the Indies, Columbus was forced to defend his actions and legal claims regarding the colony on Hispaniola. That defense was never fully published, but gathered into a collection of writings entitled, "Book of Prophecies". Columbus intended to demonstrate that his discovery of the Caribbean Islands was by God's providential plan a part of the final liberation of the Holy Land and Jerusalem from Muslim domination, leading to the end of the age and return of Jesus Christ to set up an earthly kingdom. In it, Columbus states,

"The Holy Scriptures testify in the Old Testament, by the mouth of the prophets, and in the New [Testament], by our Savior Jesus Christ, that this world will come to an end: Matthew, Mark, and Luke have recorded the signs of the end of the age; the prophets had also abundantly foretold it."

St. Augustine says that the end of this world will occur in the seventh millennium following the Creation; the sacred theologians accept his interpretation, in particular cardinal Pierre d'Ailly in Verbo XI and in other places, as I will tell below."

From the creation of the world, or from Adam, until the Advent of our Lord Jesus Christ figure 5,343 years and 318 days, by the calculation of King Alfonso

---

[121] Stephen W. Brown, Reformed Theological Seminary, Prologue, Kay Brigham (translator), "Christopher Columbus's Book of Prophecies", *Reproduction of the Original Manuscript with English Translation*, Quincentenary Edition, Libros CLIE, Spain, 1991

Who Else Believes This Is the Answer?

> *[Astronomical Tables] which is held as the most accurate…adding these figures to the approximate 1,501 years [since the birth of Christ to Columbus's time], the total is an approximate 6,845 years."*
>
> *According to this calculation, there are but 155 years left for the fulfillment of the seven thousand, at which time I have said above, by the authorities cited, that the world will come to an end."*[122]

It is clear that Columbus believed and wrote regarding the six plus seventh (sabbath) days of creation were designed to reveal 7,000 years of earth's history. It is also evident he believed the world will end, by the ordained will of God, after 7,000 years from creation. This number of 7,000 years being derived from the days of creation.

Recent Theologians

It was the result of a simple Google search. I needed to know who else held this view. Were there any other Christians who believed the days of creation were a foretelling of the ages of the earth? An internet search was easy to get to and easy to do. The result was surprising. Yes, there was a result that came back positive to the query. And, the person had written this in 1830. Just "modern" enough to imply relevance, yet enough of a historical date to give it some weight.

A Scottish literary journal from the 1830's had a short letter from a Dr. Michael Russell. It wasn't until later I was able to determine Dr. Russell was a theologian, scholar, and pastor in Scotland when he wrote the letter. Of the multiple discussions of the millennium was this gem:

> *"Their doctrine [Jews preceding the coming of Jesus Christ] in general was, that as God spent six days in the works of Creation, and rested on the seventh, and*

---

[122] Christopher Columbus, "Christopher Columbus's Book of Prophecies", *Reproduction of the Original Manuscript with English Translation*, by Kay Brigham, Quincentenary Edition, Libros CLIE, Spain, 1991, pp. 180 – 181.

> *as one day with the Almighty is as a thousand years, and a thousand years is as one day; so six thousand years would pass over mankind in toil and suffering, after which there would be a Sabbath or corresponding length to be enjoyed by the better portion of the human race – the Millennium, or thousand years of rest, peace, and happiness."*[123]

Dr. Russell's letter was in defense of a book he had written. In that book, he made a strong case against the millennium, and this reference was part of his argument.

This was a great confirmation for my burgeoning thoughts. I know. That's not what you were expecting. How could a theologian arguing against the millennium confirm my conclusion for a millennium? In three very important ways. The first was that Dr. Russell argued that the Apostles as well as early Christians were millennialists. The millennial view was a natural component of and product of their theology. Since the Apostles held this view, certainly it wouldn't be considered error. And, if this view of a millennium, and in particular the connection to the days of creation and the ages of the earth, continued in the early church, it indicates the view must have some validity. The second way Dr. Russell's letter encouraged me, was that this discussion of the millennium and relationship of the millennial reign to the days of creation was still one taken up in "modern" times. It hadn't been discarded as archaic or no longer valid. There had to be other theologians thinking and writing about this. A theology that held to this view, therefore, must have been common.

---

[123] Michael Russell, LL.D., "The Millennium, a communication from Dr. Russell", Page 78, *The Edinburgh Literary Journal; Or, Weekly Register of Criticism and Belles Lettres, Volume 3*, Ballentine and Company, No. 90, Saturday, July 31, 1830 edition. Dr. Russell is responding to criticism of his work, *Discourses On The Millennium, The Doctrine Of Election, Justification By Faith, And On The Historical Evidence For The Apostolical Institution Of episcopacy; together with some Preliminary Remarks on the Principles Of Scriptural Interpretation,* Rev. Michael Russell, LL.D., Oliver and Boyd, Edinburgh, 1830.

Who Else Believes This Is the Answer?

The third help from Dr. Russell is an illustration of a poor or wrong argument against the millennium. Dr. Russell's thesis was the belief in a millennium existed because the Apostles adopted from their Jewish heritage instead of from the clear teaching of Jesus and the revealing work of the Holy Spirit. It is clear from the disciple's question to the resurrected Jesus in Acts 1:6[124], they are looking for a physical kingdom that will exist in real space and in real time. Not an allegorical or figurative kingdom. A real kingdom. Jesus didn't answer by saying, "Foolish disciples. This is a figurative kingdom." The response of Jesus, by its lack of a rebuke of wrong thinking regarding a real kingdom, confirms a real kingdom. Therefore, when Dr. Russell argues they held this view only because they failed to properly discard discordant teaching, he makes a grave error, as would anyone using this argument. The Apostles were recipients of multiple corrective teachings during their time with Jesus. They observed and recorded the rebuke Jesus directed at the wrong teachings of the Pharisees and Scribes. Yet, correction or rebuke of this belief of a real, physical kingdom does not occur. Instead, Jesus simply tells them "It is not for you to know times or seasons that the Father has fixed by his own authority".

And, the argument against this argument (if you will) doesn't stop with that statement from Jesus. Jesus goes on to conclude this by informing the disciples of the coming indwelling Holy Spirit.[125] If the disciples had wrongly incorporated Jewish fables regarding the creation and millennium, would we not expect the Holy Spirit to instruct the Apostles and make sure this correction was incorporated and written somewhere into the New Testament writings?

---

[124] "So when they had come together, they asked him, 'Lord, will you at this time restore the kingdom to Israel?'" Acts 1:6

[125] Jesus' words conclude with, "But you will receive power when the Holy Spirit has come upon you, and you will be my witnesses in Jerusalem and in all Judea and Samaria, and to the end of the earth." Acts 1:8 And, the very clear teaching of Paul to Timothy, "All Scripture is breathed out by God and profitable for teaching, for reproof, for correction, and for training in righteousness, that the man of God may be complete, equipped for every good work." 2 Timothy 3:16-17

Other Modern Theologians

Not every modern theologian who understands eschatology from a premillennial literal return of Jesus Christ will hold this view of the answer to "Why Six Days?" I suspect that many of them have not addressed the question or would agree with the consequences of the answer. But, then, that is one of the purposes of this book.

CHAPTER 13
LIVING IN LIGHT OF THE LORD'S RETURN

What do we do? Now that we have answered this question, we must answer the question of what impact should this have on my life? For the Christian, the answer is to continue living out the Gospel in our lives more fully every day. Like the Truth of the Gospel, and every other Biblical Truth, we must let the full impact change how we think and act. We must incorporate the Truth into our daily lives which are already supposed to be characterized by never-ending worship. We need to change. But, we need to change so that we incorporate all Biblical Truth, and then live it out in front of a lost and dying world.

"But". This is how we often attempt to moderate or minimize the impact of truth. We begin with a "but", or "however", or some other way to introduce a perceived exception to the truth. We bring up a historical event that was somehow associated with the truth that ended badly. Or, resulted in heresy, or error, or just plain stupidity. And, we somehow believe this exception moderates a truth we are struggling with.

Why Six Days?

So let's face those head-on. First. No. We must not, and I fully reject any unbiblical end-of-world reaction. Fiction writers, pop-culture movie scripts, and even popular music all have end-of-world messages that may intrigue us, but have nothing to do with the real way we live. We do not sell our homes and possessions and move into the desert or into some monastery to await the Lord's return. We do not quit our jobs to spend all day preaching in the cities and become dependent on others to keep our families from starving. We do not set a date for the Lord's return and then make that date the target of all our attention. No. These are all an unbiblical responses.

Western Christian history has many examples of Christians and even pseudo-Christians who set a day for the Lord's return, and then made that day more important than the return itself. That danger and the associated damaging effect on the Gospel must be recognized and avoided. The primary defense for all of these errors is to strongly guard our affection for Jesus. Make sure we do not let His anticipated return overshadow Him. The famous day-setters are a warning against bad exegesis, losing our right affection for God, and wrongly applying partial knowledge. Along with being great examples of what not to do, they are also examples of how easy it is to fall into the trap of finding what we are looking for, and missing the real meaning and purpose God intends.

And, lest we become blind in arrogance, we should also acknowledge many who fell into the trap of setting a date in the past were intelligent, honest, and mostly well-respected individuals. They were not "cracked-pots", or "strange". If we write them off as simply foolish, and push them away with a snarky label, we will miss the important lesson of humility in knowledge. Part of their blindness may very well have been the result of a loss of humility in "knowing".

We must reject all unbiblical responses. Not just unbiblical conclusions to the answer of "Why Six Days?", but to every issue in our life. This one is no different. Our theology should be from *alpha* to *omega*, covering and addressing and impacting every part of our being and living. The way we think and what we think about. The way we speak and what we speak about. The way we act and the goals of our actions.

Since there are so many scriptures that address the second coming of Christ, how about we select one or two of those to get started?

In the letter to the church at Thessalonica, Paul gives particular encouragement that is characterized by a genuine affection and care. His theme throughout the letter has been described by multiple preachers and theologians by the title of this chapter, "Living in Light of the Lord's Return". Paul's teaching in this letter is a particularly good place to anchor our actions on the consequences of six thousand years of earth's history will be followed by the millennial reign of Jesus Christ.

Throughout the letter, Paul covers many topics that deserve our attention. As he begins to particularly address the return of Jesus, Paul encourages believers regarding those who have died after converting to Christianity. It is clear these early Christians believed their Lord would return imminently. The deaths of these fellow Christians, therefore, troubled them. Their struggle was more than a theological struggle with their eschatology. They were in emotional pain. They were hurting emotionally and spiritually. They were just like we are. One of the effects of sin is to make death painful. We miss our loved ones. It hurts to have them gone from our daily lives. Paul encourages them, reminding them it is fitting and proper that we grieve. Grieving because we miss the ones we love. Grieving because of the effect of sin that caused suffering and death. We are to grieve. But, not as those who have no hope. Our grieving is tempered by the constant truth that these loved ones will be resurrected to live in physical bodies with our Lord Jesus. We will all be resurrected and returned to our physical bodies to reign with our Savior. Paul gives them instruction on how to grieve, and reminds them of their Lord's return, and then concludes by saying,

Why Six Days?

> *Therefore encourage one another with these words.*[126]

So, here is the first thing we must do with this answer to "Why Six Days?" We are to encourage one another regarding the return of the Lord. This important and future event should be part of the way we speak to one another. When was the last time you were encouraged by another Christian regarding how to live in light of the Lord's return? How about the last time you encouraged someone about their living knowing the Lord is going to return? Not just that He will return. But, that His return impacts how we live today?

We cannot let the controversies of eschatology make us hesitant to bring up and use the certain return of Jesus Christ to reign over the earth stop us from encouraging one another. Our Savior will be physically present with us. This amazing truth should be our desire. To dwell with our Savior and God. We cannot let fear keep us from being encouraged ourselves. From speaking truth to our own souls, first. And then, to encouraging one another.

This is what Paul was doing. Christians were grieving over the deaths of their loved ones. They were beginning to wonder what would happen to their fellow Christians who had died waiting for the Lord. These early Christians fully believed the Lord would return, and expected it to be soon. Yet, they didn't know what to think about those who had become Christians, but died before the Lord returned.

There are many ways Paul could have selected to encourage and help. And, this is the one the Holy Spirit provided.

> *But we do not want you to be uninformed, brothers, about those who are asleep, that you may not grieve as others do who have no hope. For since we believe that Jesus died and rose again, even so, through Jesus, God will bring with him those who have fallen*

---

[126] 1 Thessalonians 4:18

> *asleep. For this we declare to you by a word from the Lord, that we who are alive, who are left until the coming of the Lord, will not precede those who have fallen asleep. For the Lord himself will descend from heaven with a cry of command, with the voice of an archangel, and with the sound of the trumpet of God. And the dead in Christ will rise first. Then we who are alive, who are left, will be caught up together with them in the clouds to meet the Lord in the air, and so we will always be with the Lord. Therefore encourage one another with these words.*[127]

Living in light of the Lord's return connects the resurrection of the Lord to our future hope of resurrection and fellowship with Him. Paul places that knowledge as a primary defense against wrong-living. "…since we believe that Jesus died and rose again…" This historical fact of the life, death, and resurrection of Jesus Christ is something we believe because it is true. All the events of His life, and His death, and His resurrection occurred in real physical places in clearly definable times. He had a real physical body on the earth. This real physical body died a real death like all physical bodies do. And, He was resurrected in a real physical body. Therefore, those saints who have died, and our anticipated dying, is not the final state. They, and we, will be given real physical bodies in which we can fellowship and worship and participate with Him and with one another in a coming resurrected life. This knowledge brings us great hope. Yes, we are grieved by the world and it's greater and greater rejection of God. We are deeply hurt by the impact of sin on the culture as well as creation. We see sinful things done, and it grieves us. But, we live in hope of things being put right. Of the Lord returning and making things right.

---

[127] 1 Thessalonians 4:13-18

Following this exhortation, Paul gives more instruction regarding the Lord's return, and then adds the following:

For you are all children of light, children of the day. We are not of the night or of the darkness. So then let us not sleep, as others do, but let us keep awake and be sober....Therefore encourage one another and build one another up, just as you are doing.

We ask you, brothers, to respect those who labor among you and are over you in the Lord and admonish you, and to esteem them very highly in love because of their work. Be at peace among yourselves.

And we urge you, brothers, admonish the idle, encourage the fainthearted, help the weak, be patient with them all.

See that no one repays anyone evil for evil, but always seek to do good to one another and to everyone.

Rejoice always, pray without ceasing, give thanks in all circumstances; for this is the will of God in Christ Jesus for you.

Do not quench the Spirit.

Do not despise prophecies, but test everything; hold fast what is good.

Abstain from every form of evil.[128]

Paul instructed those in Thessalonica to instruct one another with this teaching (vs. 11). We are to encourage one another and build up one another. Living in light of the Lord's return is characterized by an ongoing work of laying a foundation of doctrine that impacts our living. What we believe impacts what we do. Therefore, we must begin by laying the proper foundation of the correct doctrine. From that

---

[128] 1 Thessalonians 5:5-22

foundation of correct doctrine, we must act to produce good fruit. We move from right knowledge to right living. We cannot neglect the hard work of learning biblical doctrine and the hard work of fruitful living.

A life lived in anticipation of the Lord's return is one that is characterized by wakefulness and sobriety. We are not passive and inactive as we would be in sleep. An active person is making an impact on the world, in contrast to one that is asleep and having no impact. We are mowing our lawns and we are taking food to the neighbor who just lost a loved one to death. We are going to work, and working as unto the Lord, providing for our families and for one another. If we have debt, we are working hard to pay off that debt because this honors God and glorifies Him. We plant trees, because we know that after many years, those trees will provide fruit as God designed them to do. We are active because we are awake.

This wakefulness is characterized by being watchful. This is much more than the opposite of "asleep". The Greek word Paul used (γρηγορεύω) means awake, vigilant, or to be watchful. A person described by γρηγορεύω is more than "not sleeping." They are not being aroused from sleep and still attempting to clear their minds. This is a person who is active and being encouraged to keep awake. A command to be watchful and active.

We are to live sober lives. Clear-headed lives. Our living in anticipation of the Lord's return is characterized by sound thinking associated with reasonable judgements that produce acceptable actions. A sober person is not given to excess in worldly living. We must guard against over-indulging in those things that will keep us from being wakeful. Guard against distractions that keep us from living in anticipation of the Lord's return. Just as a person can become intoxicated with alcohol[129], and have their judgement and abilities

---

[129] An unfortunate consequence of the over-emphasis of "the evils of alcohol" in some churches is that the object (alcohol) has overshadowed other areas of intemperance. The

impaired, we can also let other things impair us. Intoxication with our work, so that it impairs. Or, an overindulgence in the culture makes us spiritual dullards. If we are known for the parties and celebrations we have around sporting events, but not for our longing for the Lord's return, we have become intemperate in our living. If we are known for having great discussions about the latest super-hero movie, but not for our encouraging one another regarding the return of Jesus, we have become intemperate.

A life lived in anticipation of the Lord's return is one that is characterized by gratitude and thankfulness (vs 18). It is a living characterized by hope and peace. This gratitude and hope produce an unquenchable desire to live a life pleasing to God. One that represents God to those around us, and one that echoes back to God the Words He spoke to us. Do you have food? Electricity? A thermostat that you can adjust to make the room a comfortable temperature? Are you dry? Clothed? We must never take for granted these things are all gifts from God. We are not entitled to any of them. Our access to a good doctor and health care that has extended our life-spans is the result of God's common grace. We do not deserve it. Be grateful.

What about friends and a good church home? If you have a pastor who faithfully preaches God's Word, and lovingly watches over your soul, be soberly purposeful to express your gratitude (vs. 12-13). First to God. But, also to your pastor. This is living in light of the return of your Lord. When you pastor speaks God's truth to you with the authority God has given him, respond in a manner that confesses your pastor is carrying out his God-ordained ministry which is the charge of God on him to care for you. And, be grateful.

---

irony that the resistance to this single thing is often characterized by an intemperate emphasis should point toward the need to be truly temperate in all things. Even in our intemperance.

Living in Light of the Lord's Return

In addition to watching out over our own lives, and being grateful for the shepherds God has placed over us, we must purposefully care for one another (vs 14). My own Pastor, Kevin Boling, in expositing this verse, noted this passage takes the responsibility for soul care we normally place on a pastor and extends it to the entire body of Christ.[130] In contradiction to the wrongful question of Cain when God asked him about the state of his brother, Abel, "We *are* our brother's keeper." This does not mean we are to take up every social cause. Real soul care for our brothers in Christ, and concern for our unsaved neighbors, means we must reject the world's version of being "our brother's keeper" which makes the needy dependent on the hand out of someone else. We must encourage and lift them into proper care for themselves so they can also begin caring for another person.

For the fellow Christian, though, the requirement is greater. To do what Paul instructs requires that we become skilled and willing to provide good soul care for one another. It means we must study to discern whether a brother in Christ is simply weak, or if they are in rebellion or disorderly. I must know God's Word well, so that the truth of His Word can be used by the Holy Spirit to inform my intellect regarding the genuine need. This is not a simple or easy task. It is one that requires wakefulness and sobriety. It is one that requires a constant reminder that our Lord is standing at the door. He is not distant. His return is soon. Whether you and I are confronting an unruly or out-of-rank brother in Christ, or lifting the head of a sister wounded by the words of a family member, we do so with the ever-present awareness of the immediate presence of our Savior and Lord Jesus Christ. We live as if His return is imminent because His return is imminent.

This knowledge, this answer to "Why Six Days, followed by a Day of Rest?" reminds us that time is not immeasurable. It has been measured by the very God who created time. The span of the existence

---

[130] Kevin Boling, sermon on 1 Thessalonians 5:14, Mountain Bridge Bible Church, Travelers Rest, SC, March 18, 2018.

of the universe is in His hand. He is the *alpha* and the *omega*. Unlike the creation, the Creator is eternal. Our limited time in this creation is only part of His eternal purpose and plan. But, it is a limited time.

---

[131] Headpiece to the Book of Revelation, Macklinburg Bible, By Phillip Medhurst (Photos by Harry Kossuth) [Public domain], via Wikimedia Commons, https://upload.wikimedia.org/wikipedia/commons/b/b3/Vignette_by_Loutherbourg_for_the_Macklin_Bible_133_of_134._Bowyer_Bible_New_Testament._Headpiece_to_Revelations.gif

Why Six Days?

Scripture References

1 Corinthians 15:20, 79
1 Corinthians 16:2, 92
1 Corinthians 5:7, 78
1 John 2:27, 81
1 Peter 1:17-21, 79
1 Thessalonians 4:13-18, 116, 145
1 Thessalonians 4:18, 144
1 Thessalonians 4:7, 78
1 Thessalonians 5:5-22, 146
2 Timothy 3:16-17, 139
Acts 1:6, 118, 139
Acts 2:1-4, 80
Acts 20:7, 92
Colossians 3:23-24, 58
Daniel 9:25, 49
Exodus 14, 63
Exodus 17:1-7, 100
Exodus 20:8-11, 57, 92
Exodus 23:10-11, 67
Exodus 28:30, 35
Exodus 3 – 13, 63
Exodus 31:13-17, 94
Genesis 1:28, 106, 122
Genesis 12:1-3, 123
Genesis 2:7, 25
Genesis 7:1-4, 59
Genesis 8:10-12, 62
Genesis 8:5-9, 61
Hebrews 4:1, 101
Hebrews 4:4-11, 102
Isaiah 46:8-1, 7
Isaiah 53:3-9, 113
Jeremiah 23:1-8, 108
Jeremiah 25:8-12, 108
Jeremiah 31:33, 80
Job 19:25-27, 115
John 1:1-3, 25
John 1:1-4, 4
John 2:18-19, 43
John 2:20-22, 44
John 20, 92
Leviticus 23:1-3, 75
Leviticus 23:23-25, 82
Leviticus 23:27-31, 83
Leviticus 23:39-43, 84
Leviticus 25:23-28, 70
Leviticus 25:8, 68
Luke 24, 92
Mark 16, 92
Mark 2:27-28, 89
Matthew 12:6-8, 46
Matthew 18:15-20, 43
Matthew 19:3-6, 26
Matthew 24:2, 117
Matthew 24:3, 117
Matthew 28, 92
Philippians 4:2-3, 128
Psalms 95:7-9, 100
Revelation 13:8, 81
Revelation 2:29, 50
Revelation 20:1-6, 27
Revelation 20:1-7, 120
Zechariah 12:10-14, 112
Zechariah 14:16, 111
Zechariah 14:4, 110
Zechariah 14:9, 110

ABOUT THE AUTHOR

Dr. Marks is a Professor of Chemistry at a Christian University in South Carolina where he has taught courses in Chemistry, Earth Science, Physics, and Honors Seminars. He has served as an Elder, Music Leader, and Sunday School teacher in local churches. Dr. Marks is blessed to have been married to Joann Williams since 1981. They have one amazing treasure of a daughter.

Before teaching Chemistry at his current school, Dr. Marks spent twenty years in the United States Air Force, where he served his country managing the acquisition of aircraft simulators, leading and participating in chemical and biological intelligence work, and teaching at the United States Air Force Academy. At the Air Force Academy, Dr. Marks directed their largest chemical education course, with 20 faculty teaching over 1,000 students each semester. Ron retired in the rank of Major in 2002.

Ron was licensed to preach by First Southern Baptist Church of Cortez, Colorado. He has served as an ordained deacon in Baptist and independent conservative Churches in Colorado, and as an ordained lay minister in Tennessee, Colorado, Florida, and South Carolina. He also is a speaker on Creation issues, and has taught courses on Creation in local churches.

Dr. Marks earned three academic degrees from the University of Tennessee at Knoxville: Bachelor of Arts in Chemistry (Honors, 1982), Master of Science in Chemistry (1988), and Doctor of Philosophy in Chemistry (1994). He is a member of the Creation Research Society and the Military Officers Association of America. His research interests include the study of creation, the relationship of science and Christianity, computational chemistry, and novel stereoselective synthesis.

Why Six Days?

Made in the USA
Columbia, SC
26 May 2025